Functioning in Business

NEW EDITION

P. Lance Knowles and Francis Bailey

with Rosi Jillett

Longman

London and New York

Longman Group UK Ltd.
Longman House, Burnt Mill, Harlow
Essex CM20 2JE, England
and Associated companies throughout the world

Published in the United States of America by Longman Inc., New York

First published 1987
New edition 1991
ISBN 0 582 06161. X

Set in Linotype Ehrhardt, 11/13pt
Produced by Longman Group (FE) Ltd
Printed in Hong Kong

CONTENTS

The **Answer Key** is a separate supplement in the back of the book.

PREFACE

This text was developed over three years working with students in the intensive English program at the Language Institute of Japan. Our need was to improve our program in two areas: language functions useful for managing simple conversations in business, and listening comprehension. Though there were ample materials available for intermediate and advanced learners, we were not satisfied with existing materials designed for pre-intermediate learners.

Our working assumptions were as follows:

1. language should be in context, preferably in a developing story of interest to adult learners, especially those involved in business;
2. at pre-intermediate levels, listening activities should play an especially important role in promoting language acquisition;
3. students should move from recognition and comprehension to *eventual* production and acquisition;
4. language functions and simple routines should be systematically recycled throughout the materials;
5. written follow-up exercises should help students recognize key phrases and should require listening for comprehension, first for gist and then for details.

With these assumptions as our guide, we identified what we felt to be the key language functions appropriate for pre-intermediate learners. We then developed a story within which these functions would naturally occur. Once the story took shape, we asked members of our staff to role play the situations (with no script). The results had an authentic quality that found positive acceptance by our students, so we were on our way.

Though the language level of the material seemed high at first, we isolated the points in each unit which caused difficulty and designed pre-listening and other exercises to guide students through the rough spots. We also added the introductory unit as a means to reduce the learning load. During the role plays it became clear which functions the students needed to work on, and gradually, as students progressed through the text, our target phrases came to be incorporated into student speech. At the same time, much of the vocabulary which had seemed difficult for the students in the first episodes was steadily acquired, so that the text became easier (requiring less class time) as the term progressed. This allowed us to increase the difficulty of the variations. Used in this way, student progress was clear to both students and teachers, and the materials evolved into an integrated course, not just a series of unrelated lessons.

Acknowledgement

We would like to thank the following people for their assistance in developing the material: Brian Tobin, Laura Mayer, Michael Curtin, Dave Pickles, Chris Dickinson, and Naoko Seto.

We would like to thank the entire staff of the Language Institute of Japan for their support and encouragement throughout this project. In particular, we would like to thank Meg Grace, Paul Lehnert, Ellen Dussourd, Andy Gates, Duncan Macintyre, Kathy Maston, and Larry Riesberg.

Finally, we would like to thank Robert O'Neill and Steven Krashen, whose somewhat differing views influenced us in the preparation of these materials.

Lance Knowles
Francis Bailey

Picture Acknowledgements

We would like to thank Images Colour Library Ltd for their permission to reproduce copyright photographs on pages 32 and 53 of this textbook.

All other photographs by Gary Trippeer and Dick Castledine. Cover photograph by Gary Trippeer.

USING THE COURSE

Rationale

Functioning in Business is for pre-intermediate students preparing to use English in a business context. In addition to basic vocabulary and concepts, it is important at this stage to develop a working knowledge of essential language functions (e.g. requesting, suggesting, refusing, etc.), without which it is almost impossible to manage even a simple conversation. The approach taken here is to develop students in two areas; recognition of key functional phrases, and production of key functional phrases. By "recognition" we mean that students comprehend the message or intent of a phrase but may not be able to generate that phrase for spoken production. We use "production" to mean that students can do both. In order to develop proficiency in both areas, key phrases are recycled from unit to unit and in a variety of situations.

The second major area of focus is on listening, both for general meaning and for specific items of information. Units are organized into pre-listening, general listening, and detailed listening sections. Once these sections have been completed, students will have an understanding of the contextualized content of the conversations. The focus of the unit then shifts from information and content to how the conversation itself is actually managed and to the key functional phrases.

The third aim of this text is to build a basic business vocabulary. Terminology specific to particular technical fields is avoided as much as possible, our aim being to concentrate on recycling high-frequency items that are essential in general business conversations. The core vocabulary of the book is recycled so that the book becomes increasingly easy as students progress.

In order to help students reach the "production" stage more effectively, this new edition has introduced more explicit presentation material so students are taken through the stages of presentation, controlled practice and then freer production of the key functional phrases. The material is designed with audio and video users equally in mind. Ideas for further video exploitation (including how to present key functional phrases) are given in the Teacher's Guide.

The Materials

The complete Course consists of a Students' Book, a Teacher's Guide and a video or audio cassette. It can be used both in the classroom and for self-access, although in the latter case, student involvement in the material may be less for lack of an opportunity to do the role plays.

Each unit consists of a series of exercises that establish the basic information and context of each Episode. These are followed by the Functional Phrases section, which (re-)presents and practices a mixture of familiar and new phrases. In the Role Play, students demonstrate both their comprehension of the total situation and their ability to use appropriate functional phrases from previously acquired language. The exercises in the Variation section feature the same or similar phrases but in a different situation (one unrelated to the main storyline).

The Answer Key in the back of the Students' Book includes answers to the General Comprehension and Detailed Listening sections, the transcripts of the Episode dialogs and of the Variations.

INTRODUCTION

Part 1

This is the story of an important business trip. It begins with two companies, Yamashita Ltd. and Advanced Technologies.

1. *Look at the pictures below. What do they tell you about the two companies?*

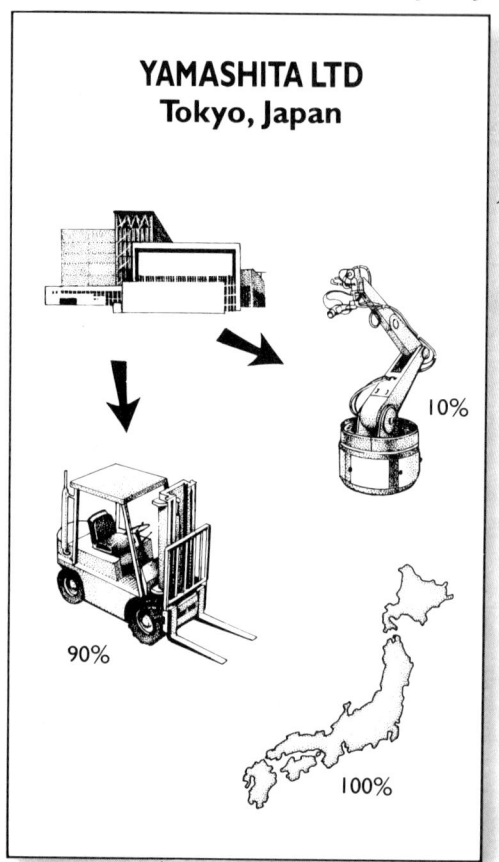

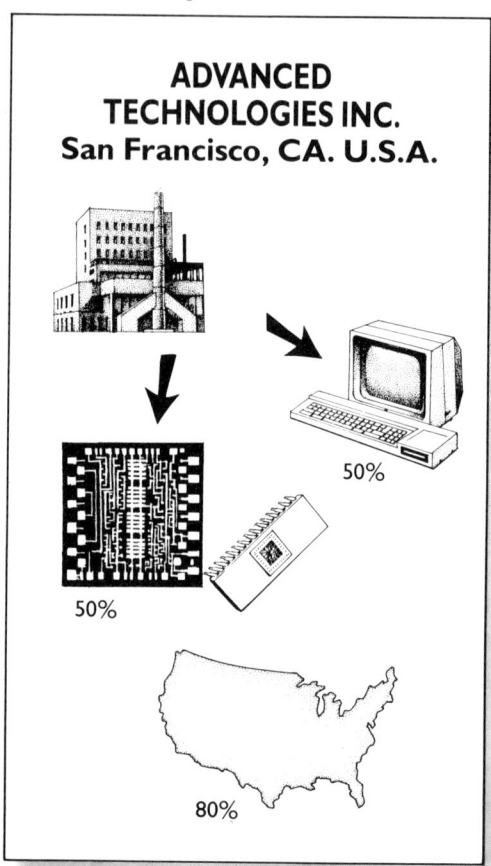

2. *Now listen to the cassette and complete the table below.*

	CHARLES BLAKE	MIKE EPSTEIN
COMPANY	*Yamashita*	
MAIN OFFICE		*San Francisco*
PRODUCTS		
MAIN MARKET		
SECONDARY MARKET		*Overseas and Canada*

Part 2

The main characters in this story are Charles Blake and Mike Epstein. Here is information about them.

1. *Look at the pictures, and listen to the tape. Mark the sentences below each picture true (T) or false (F).*

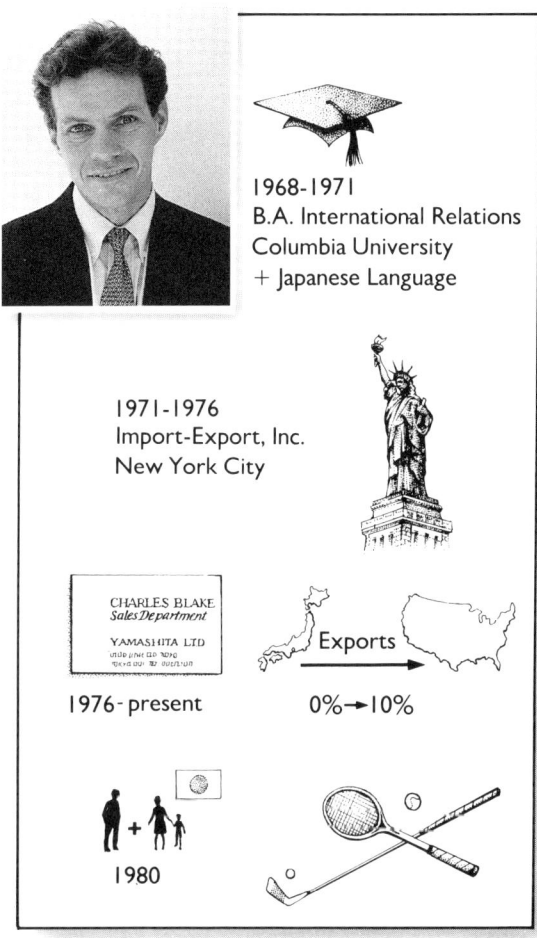

a. Mr. Blake is an engineer.	a. Mr. Epstein is an engineer.
b. Mr. Blake works in New York.	b. Mr. Epstein works in San Francisco.
c. Mr. Blake is married.	c. Mr. Epstein is married.
d. Mr. Blake works for a Japanese company.	d. Mr. Epstein works for a Japanese company.

2. *Listen again.*

a. What are Charles Blake's and Mike Epstein's responsibilities?

b. What are your responsibilities?

3. *Imagine you are at a meeting, sitting around a table. You are asked to introduce yourself and your company briefly. What do you say?*

Part 3

The story began two months ago, in April. The pictures below give you some information. What do you think happened?

1. *Now listen to the tape to find out exactly what happened. How similar was your story to the one you have just heard?*

2. *Mark the sentences below true (T) or false (F). Listen again if you are not sure.*

a. Mr. Epstein went to Japan on vacation.   T   F
b. Mr. Epstein attended the trade show in Tokyo to sell office computers.   T   F
c. Mr. Blake is going to come to San Francisco.   T   F
d. Mr. Blake is going to be in San Francisco from June 11th to June 13th only.   T   F
e. Mr. Epstein and Mr. Blake are going to meet in San Francisco.   T   F
f. Mr. Epstein is definitely going to place an order for industrial robots from Yamashita.   T   F

Checking In

A. Story Update

How much do you remember from the introduction?

1. Who is the man on the right of the photograph?
2. What company does he work for?
3. Why is he in San Francisco?

Now listen to the story update to check your answers.

B. Pre-Listening

You are traveling alone on a business trip to the United States. You want to check in to a hotel.

How do you usually solve each of the following problems? (Rank the choices from 1–4 to indicate the order of your preferences.)

1. You book your hotel room
   a. with a confirmed reservation by a travel agency.
   b. by personal letter.
   c. by calling from the airport.
   d. when you arrive at the hotel.

2. The kind of room you usually stay in is a
   a. single.
   b. twin.
   c. double.
   d. suite.

3. When you check in, the first thing you want to confirm is
   a. the check-out time.
   b. the room rate.
   c. how you will pay.
   d. if you have any messages.

4. You usually pay by
   a. cash.
   b. personal check.
   c. traveler's check.
   d. major credit card.

5. The most popular international credit cards in your country are
   a. VISA.
   b. American Express.
   c. Master Card.
   d. another kind of credit card.

C. General Comprehension

Listen to the dialog and mark these sentences true (T) or false (F).

1. Charles Blake has a reservation for the hotel.   T F
2. The hotel clerk cannot find Mr. Blake's reservation.   T F
3. The reservation is for one night only.   T F
4. Mr. Blake would like to pay with cash.   T F
5. Mr. Blake wants to leave a day early.   T F
6. There are a number of rooms available on Friday night. T F

D. Detailed Listening

Listen again and fill in this hotel registration form.

> # *Embassy Suites*
> # *Hotel*
>
> NAME ....
>
> RESERVATION NUMBER ....
>
> DATE OF ARRIVAL ....
>
> DATE OF DEPARTURE ....
>
> ROOM NUMBER ....
>
> PRICE OF ROOM ....
>
> METHOD OF PAYMENT
> Cash/Credit Card*
> Credit Card details ....
>
> *Delete as appropriate

E. Functional Phrases

1. *Check these words in your dictionary if you are not sure what they mean.*

AGREE   CONFIRM   OFFER   REFUSE   REQUEST

2. *Match the words and phrases in Column A to the phrases in Column B.*

A

a. agreeing
b. confirming
c. refusing
d. making a request
e. making a very polite request
f. offering

B

i.   Is that correct?
ii.   Yes, that's fine.
iii. If you could do that, I'd really appreciate it.
iv.   Can I use my American Express card?
v.   Yes, certainly.
vi.   Can I help you?
vii. I'm afraid we're all booked up.

Offering, Confirming, Agreeing

3. *Look at the text. Try to complete the sentences with phrases from Column B above. Then check your answers by listening to the dialog.*

CLERK: Good evening, sir. Welcome to the Embassy Suites Hotel. _____

BLAKE: Yeah, my name is Blake, Charles Blake.

I have a confirmed reservation.

CLERK: Mr. Blake. Yes. And the reservation number?

BLAKE: Let's see. Er, here it is—14689.

CLERK: 14689. Let me check. Yes, sir. We have your reservation right here.

That's for June 10th through the 13th, Monday through Thursday night.

_____, sir?

BLAKE: _____

Requesting, Agreeing, Refusing

4. *Now listen to the second part of the dialog and complete it.*

CLERK: That room is $120 a night.

BLAKE: Okay, fine. _____ use my American Express card for that?

CLERK: _____, sir. _____ print of your card before

            we check you in?

            . . . .

BLAKE: Oh, by the way, there's a chance I will be staying one more day, so I might be leaving

            on Saturday. Is that okay?

CLERK: Let me check. Well sir, _____ we're all booked up for Friday

            night, but something may open up. Can I let you know?

BLAKE: Okay, _____ let me know as soon as possible,

            _____

CLERK: Yes, we can do that for you, sir. Okay, and here's your key, sir. I'll get the bellman.

            Bellman, front!

F.   Role Play

Work in pairs. Take turns role playing parts A and B below. The situation is the same as above. Then listen to the dialog again.

Part A

You are checking into the Embassy Suites Hotel. It is June 10th. Use your own name. Your reservation number is 14689, and you want to stay an extra night until Saturday, June 15th.

Part B

You are the hotel clerk at the Embassy Suites Hotel. Please help A, who has reserved a room through Thursday night. The hotel is fully booked on Friday.

Variation: Cashing a Check

Comprehension

Listen to the dialog and answer the questions.

1.	Can the customer change British pounds for American dollars?	Yes/No
2.	Can the customer cash a personal check?	Yes/No
3.	Can the customer see the manager?	Yes/No
4.	Does the customer agree to see the Assistant Manager, Ms. Grace?	Yes/No

Functional Phrases

Could I	May I help you?	Could I
I'm sorry but	I'm afraid	Can I
		Yes. That's fine

Try to complete the text with phrases from the box above. Then check your answers by listening to the dialog.

BANK TELLER: _____

CUSTOMER: Yes. _____ change British pounds for American dollars here?

BANK TELLER: Yes, certainly, sir. How much would you like to change?

CUSTOMER: One hundred pounds please. Also, _____ cash this personal check from my London bank?

BANK TELLER: _____ that isn't possible. Our policy is that we do not cash out of town checks.

CUSTOMER: It's very important that I cash this check . . .

BANK TELLER: Yes, I understand, but the bank policy . . .

CUSTOMER: _____ see the manager please?

BANK TELLER: _____ the manager, Mr. Grover, is out right now. The Assistant Manager, Ms. Grace is in. Would that be all right?

CUSTOMER: _____ Thank you.

BANK TELLER: Certainly. One moment please.

Now practice role playing the variation.

Making an Appointment

A. Story Update

Look at the photograph.

1. Where is Charles Blake?
2. Who do you think he is phoning? Why?

Now listen to the story update to check your answers.

B.   Pre-Listening

Rank your choices 1–3.

1.   Mr. Blake is going to telephone Mr. Epstein. What do you think they will discuss?

    a.   the objective of the meeting
    b.   the time and place of the meeting
    c.   the price of the robots

2.   When will Epstein and Blake probably meet?

    a.   today
    b.   tomorrow
    c.   next week

3.   Where do you think Blake and Epstein will meet?

    a.   at Epstein's office
    b.   at Blake's hotel
    c.   at a restaurant

C.   General Comprehension

Listen to the dialog.
Were your choices in 'B' correct?

D.   Detailed Listening

Listen again and complete Charles Blake's diary entries for June 11th and 12th. Make notes in as much detail as possible about who *he will meet,* where, when, *and* why.

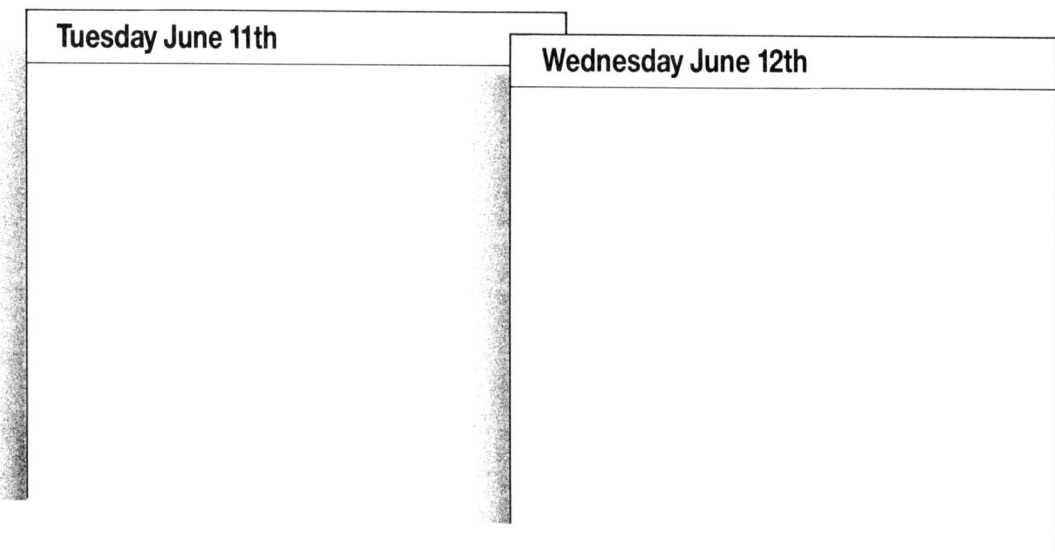

Tuesday June 11th

Wednesday June 12th

E. Functional Phrases

1. *Study this table.*

OFFERING	May I help you?
INTRODUCING	This is . . .
GREETING	How are you? I'm fine, thanks.
REQUESTING	I'd like to speak with . . .

2. *Try to complete the text with phrases from the table above. Then check your answers by listening to the dialog.*

RECEPTIONIST: Advanced Technologies. _____

BLAKE: Yes. _____ Charles Blake from Yamashita Limited _____ Mike Epstein, please.

RECEPTIONIST: Just a minute and I'll put you through.

. . . .

EPSTEIN: Mr. Blake.

BLAKE: Hello, Mr. Epstein. _____

EPSTEIN: _____ How are you?

BLAKE: Great. I had a nice flight and it was on time.

EPSTEIN: When did you get in to San Francisco?

BLAKE: I just arrived a few moments ago.

3. *In the next part of the conversation, Mike Epstein suggests they meet. Does he say:*
   a. Say, when shall we get together?
   b. Well, when can I see you?
   c. Say, why don't we get together?

4. *Charles Blake says "Well, I was hoping that we could perhaps arrange a meeting for tomorrow sometime."*

    Does he mean:

    a.   I wanted to meet you tomorrow, but now I realize this won't be possible?
    b.   I would like to meet you tomorrow?

5. *Mike Epstein suggests they meet after 11:00 and wants to know if this is convenient for Charles Blake. How does he ask him?*

    I'm free after eleven o'clock. _____?

6. *After they arrange to meet Mike Epstein mentions a meeting with Shirley Graham. How does he introduce this new topic?*

    Great. Uh, just _____.

7. *Mike Epstein suggests a meeting with Shirley Graham on Wednesday. What does he say?*

    I was wondering if we could get together again, _____ Wednesday?

8. *What does Blake say to confirm the time and the place?*

    Okay. _____.

F.   Role Play

Work in groups of three. Take turns role playing parts A, B, and C below. The situation is the same as above. Then listen to the dialog again.

Part A	Part B	Part C
Make an appointment to see C at Advanced Technologies. You are staying at the Embassy Suites Hotel. You would like to see C as soon as possible. You work for Yamashita Ltd. Confirm the time and place of meeting.	You are the receptionist at Advanced Technologies.	You are expecting A's call. You want to meet A tomorrow morning and you want A to meet with your boss, Shirley Graham, on Wednesday. Confirm the details of the meeting. Your office is near the Embassy Suites hotel.

Variation 1: Making an Appointment

Read the telephone dialog below. Choose the best answer for each blank. Then listen to check your answers.

BLISS: Webber Industries, may I help you?

MILTON: Yes. _____

        a.   This is Roberta Milton.   b.   This is Ms. Milton.

BLISS: This is Sam Bliss speaking. How are you Ms. Milton?

MILTON: _____

        a.   Fine and you?   b.   How are you?

BLISS: Just fine, thank you.

MILTON: I'm calling to see if we can arrange a meeting. There are several matters I'd like to discuss with you.

BLISS: Okay, when would be convenient?

MILTON: _____

        a.   I want to meet with you tomorrow.   b.   Could we meet tomorrow?

BLISS: Yes, that's possible. What time would be convenient?

MILTON: _____

        a.   How about 2:30?   b.   I'd like to see you at 2:30.

BLISS: Fine. I'm looking forward to seeing you.

MILTON: Me too. Okay, in your office at 2:30 tomorrow, right?

BLISS: Right. See you then.

MILTON: See you tomorrow.

Variation 2: Leaving a Message

Listen to the dialog and write in the exact words.

RECEPTIONIST: Webber Industries, _____?

MILTON: _____ from Myer's Shipping Company.

                 _____?

RECEPTIONIST: _____ Mr. Webber is not here right now. Can I take a

                 message?

MILTON: Yes. Could you please ask Mr. Webber to call me back before 5:00 today?

RECEPTIONIST: Yes of course. _____?

MILTON: Certainly. M-I-L-T-O-N.

RECEPTIONIST: _____?

MILTON: Yes. 877-3088.

Practice role playing Variation 1 and Variation 2. Use your real name, but take the position of the characters in the story.

Confirming Plans

A.   Story Update

Listen to the story update and answer the questions.

1.   Who is Shirley Graham?
2.   What very important entry is in Shirley Graham's diary for October?

B. Pre-Listening

Before you listen to the dialog, answer the following questions.

1. Why does Epstein want to talk with Graham?

2. What questions are the most important for Epstein to confirm?
    (Rank your choices from 1–3.)

    a. Is she free for the meeting?
    b. What is the purpose of the meeting?
    c. When and where should they meet?

3. Mike Epstein probably _____ to buy industrial robots from Yamashita Ltd.
    (Circle your choice.)

    a. wants
    b. doesn't want

4. At tomorrow's meeting, Ms. Graham wants
    (Rank your choices from 1–3.)

    a. to learn more about Yamashita Ltd.
    b. to discuss problems.
    c. to get to know Mr. Blake.

5. Yamashita Ltd. has no experience in North America. As a result, what kind of problems might they have in selling their robots in the U.S.? *(Rank your choices from 1–3.)*

    a. high shipping costs
    b. providing service and spare parts
    c. advertising and marketing

6. Do you think that Shirley Graham

    a. answers all Epstein's points?
    b. stalls (i.e. she says let's discuss these points at tomorrow's meeting)?
    c. is not interested in discussing Epstein's points?

C. General Comprehension

Now listen to the dialog and mark these sentences true (T) or false (F).

1. Ms. Graham cannot meet Mr. Blake because she's too busy.   T   F
2. Ms. Graham wants to change the time of the meeting.   T   F
3. Epstein had a good meeting with Blake earlier today.   T   F
4. Epstein is against buying robots from Yamashita.   T   F
5. Graham thinks there are some problems.   T   F

D. Detailed Listening

Now listen to the dialog once more and complete the following sentences.

1. Epstein and Graham will leave their office at _____ tomorrow.

    a. 11:45
    b. 12:00
    c. 12:15

2. Epstein is going to pick up Graham at

    a. her office.
    b. Blake's hotel.
    c. his office.

3. Graham is worried about the problem of

    a. high shipping costs.
    b. aftersales service and the October deadline.
    c. advertising and marketing.

4. Mike Epstein thinks that

    a. there isn't a problem.
    b. Yamashita's technology is excellent.
    c. they should decide not to buy robots from Yamashita Ltd.

5. Graham says "Yes. All right. Let's discuss it further tomorrow." In this conversation, this means:

    a. I agree. Lct's discuss it further tomorrow.
    b. I don't agree and I don't want to discuss it further.
    c. I understand, but I don't want to discuss it now.

E. Functional Phrases

Requesting, Offering, Confirming

1. *Study this table.*

REQUESTING	. . . do you have a minute?
OFFERING	Have a seat.
CONFIRMING	. . . sounds just fine. That's right.

2. *Complete the dialog using the phrases you looked at in Exercise 1. Then listen to check your answers.*

GRAHAM: Come in.

EPSTEIN: Oh, Shirley, _____

GRAHAM: Sure. Come on in Mike. _____

EPSTEIN: Oh, thanks. Listen, I just wanted to let you know that I've made reservations for lunch tomorrow afternoon at 12:15. Okay?

GRAHAM: With Mr. Blake?

EPSTEIN: _____ of Yamashita Limited.

GRAHAM: Okay. So, we should leave here at . . .?

EPSTEIN: About 12:00.

GRAHAM: 12:00 _____

EPSTEIN: I'll pick you up here at 12 o'clock and we can go to his hotel together.

Disagreeing Politely, Giving an Opinion, Stalling

3. a. *Put the phrases below into pairs so that each pair has a similar meaning.*

   I can see why you don't agree with what I'm saying, but . . .
   Let's discuss it further tomorrow.
   In my opinion . . .
   I don't think that this is the best time to talk about it.
   I understand your reservations, but . . .
   I think . . .

   b. *Now put each pair under the correct heading:*

DISAGREEING POLITELY	GIVING AN OPINION	STALLING

4. *In their meeting Shirley Graham and Mike Epstein use one phrase from each heading in Exercise 3. Which ones do you think they use?*
   Now listen and complete the dialog.

EPSTEIN: Yes, I did, and again I was very impressed with his flexibility and his . . .

_____ that we can work things out with him.

GRAHAM: Okay. As long as it's clear to both of you that it has to be worked out, and before

October, because that's our deadline.

EPSTEIN: Well, again, _____ Shirley,

but again the technology of their product is really excellent. I think we really have to

go ahead with this.

GRAHAM: Yes. All right. Well, _____

All right?

EPSTEIN: Okay. All right. Thank you. We'll see you tomorrow.

GRAHAM: We'll see you around 12:00.

EPSTEIN: Okay.

F. Role Play

Work in pairs. Take turns role playing parts A and B below. The situation is the same as above. Then listen to the dialog again.

Part A

In this short meeting with your boss, B, confirm the details for tomorrow's meeting with Charles Blake. You are in favor of buying robots from Yamashita, and you hope B will agree.

Part B

You are worried about several problems with Yamashita. You and A are going to meet with Mr. Blake of Yamashita Ltd. tomorrow. You need to confirm the details of the meeting with A.

Variation 1: Checking an Appointment

Here are two parts of a dialog. Read the part on the left (Mrs. Powers' part).
Now find the correct order for the part on the right (Mr. Malone's part).
After you have finished, listen to the dialog and check your answer.

Powers

1. Excuse me. Do you have a minute?
2. Thanks. I made an appointment for us to see Mr. Myers. Are you still free at 11:00 on Wednesday?
3. That's too bad.
4. That's fine with me.
5. Sure. I'll call him right away.

Malone

a. How about 1:00 on Friday?
b. Would you call him back and see if Friday is good for him?
c. 11:00 on Wednesday? I'm afraid not. I'm busy all morning.
d. Thanks.
e. Certainly. Please come in.

Variation 2: Changing an Appointment

Read the dialog below. Choose the best answer for each blank. Then listen to check your answers.

MYERS: Hello. _____ Bob Myers speaking.

     a. I am   b. This is

POWERS: Hello, this is Sandra Powers from Delta Electronics. _____ but Mr. Malone is busy on Wednesday.

     a. I'm afraid   b. I'm sorry   c. I'm sorry, I'm afraid

     If it's _____ for you, could we change our appointment to 1:00 on Friday?

     a. convenient   b. right

MYERS: _____ that you're very busy, but Friday is too late. We have some very serious problems.

     a. I think   b. I understand

     _____ we should meet as soon as possible.

     a. I think   b. I understand

POWERS: I see. _____ I call you back later today? I want to check our schedule for Thursday.

     a. I want   b. Could

MYERS: Good. I'll be expecting your call later today.

Now practice role playing the variations.

An Important Introduction

A. Story Update

1. Why is Mr. Blake going to meet Ms. Graham?
2. What kind of problems is Shirley Graham probably worried about?
3. Why do you think Shirley Graham is worried about doing business with a foreign company?

Now listen to the story update to check your answers.

B. Pre-Listening

Before you listen to the dialog, answer the following questions.

1. What are the relationships among Blake, Epstein, and Graham?
    Match the names with the correct description.

    Blake and Epstein   a. They have never met.
    Graham and Epstein   b. They are old friends.
    Graham and Blake   c. They have met several times on business and have played
                                   golf together.
                               d. They work together in the same company. She is his
                                   boss.

2. *Circle the correct form/s of address in this situation.*

    Mike Epstein addresses Charles Blake as: Mr. Blake/Charles

    Mike Epstein addresses Shirley Graham as: Ms. Graham/Shirley

    Shirley Graham addresses Mike Epstein as: Mr. Epstein/Mike

    Shirley Graham addresses Charles Blake as: Mr. Blake/Charles

    Charles Blake addresses Shirley Graham as: Ms. Graham/Shirley

    Charles Blake addresses Mike Epstein as: Mr. Epstein/Mike

3. After introductions, the first thing they will discuss is
    (*Rank your choices from 1 – 3.*)

    a. the weather.
    b. business.
    c. Mr. Blake's trip.

4. Who arranged this meeting?

5. Who is the most important person at this meeting?

C. General Comprehension

Listen to the dialog and mark these sentences true (T) or false (F).

1. They discussed business right after the introductions.   T   F
2. This is Blake's first trip to San Francisco.   T   F
3. They are going to have lunch together.   T   F
4. They are going to eat lunch in the hotel.   T   F

D. Detailed Listening

Listen again and answer the following questions.

1. When Mike Epstein introduced Shirley Graham to Charles Blake he gave

    a.   her name and her position in the company.
    b.   her position in the company.
    c.   the name of the company, her name and position in the company.

2. How long ago was Blake in San Francisco?

    a.   This is his first trip to San Francisco.
    b.   He was in San Francisco seven years ago.
    c.   He was in San Francisco for a brief visit.

3. Yesterday Charles Blake

    a.   went to Fisherman's Wharf with an old friend.
    b.   saw a bit of San Francisco with Mike Epstein.
    c.   visited the West Coast for the first time.

4. Last time Blake was in San Francisco, he stayed

    a.   for about the same length of time as this time.
    b.   for only a day or two.
    c.   for a week or longer.

5. Mike Epstein interrupts the conversation because

    a.   they have a reservation at a restaurant.
    b.   he wants to continue the conversation.
    c.   they are going to walk to a restaurant.

E. Functional Phrases

Introducing and Greeting

1. *In this episode Mike Epstein introduces Shirley Graham to Charles Blake, and they all greet each other.*
    We use different expressions to greet people. Study the table below.

GREETING SOMEONE FOR THE FIRST TIME	Pleased to meet you. It's nice to meet you. How do you do?
GREETING SOMEONE YOU KNOW	It's good to see you. How are you?

2. *Try to complete the dialog. Then listen and write the exact words.*

BLAKE: Oh, hi, Mike. _____ today?

EPSTEIN: _____ Charles. _____

our Vice-President, Shirley Graham. Shirley, _____ Charles

Blake from Yamashita Ltd.

GRAHAM: _____, Mr. Blake.

BLAKE: _____, Ms. Graham.

GRAHAM: _____

BLAKE: _____

GRAHAM: Just fine. Mike tells me that . . .

3. *When do we say "It's nice to meet you"?*
   Is it usually:

   a. while we shake hands?
   b. before we shake hands?
   c. after we have shaken hands?

   Do people shake hands in your country?

4. *Introduce the following people to each other.*

a.	NAME	Dr. Kramer	Mr. Kirihara
	POSITION	Human Resources Manager	Training Manager
	COMPANY	ICI	Toyota

b.	NAME	Ms. Brooke	Mrs. Lee
	POSITION	Purchasing Officer	Sales Manager
	COMPANY	Siemens	IBM

Interrupting, Suggesting, Agreeing

5. *Listen and write the exact words.*

EPSTEIN: Well, _____ but we have a car outside and we have

reservations at 12:15. So _____ get over to the restaurant and

we can continue our conversation there.

GRAHAM: Okay.

EPSTEIN: Okay?

BLAKE: _____ to me.

EPSTEIN: Okay. _____

F.   Role Play

Work in groups of three. Take turns role playing parts A, B, and C below. The situation is the same as above. Then listen to the dialog again.

Part A

You are in Blake's role. You had a good time with B yesterday, and you are looking forward to meeting C.

Part B

You are in Epstein's role. Introduce C to A, and act as the host. You have made reservations for lunch.

Part C

You are in Graham's role. Welcome A to San Francisco, and ask questions about A's trip.

Variation 1: Introducing Yourself

Bob Myers comes to the office of Delta Electronics. Mrs. Powers comes down to the reception area and introduces herself.

Read the dialog below. Choose the best answers for each blank. Then listen to check your answers.

POWERS: Mr. Myers?

MYERS: Yes. _____

a.   That's right.   b.   And you?

POWERS: _____ Sandra Powers. I work with Mr. Malone.

    a. I'm . . .   b. This is . . .

MYERS: Mrs. Powers. _____ I've been looking forward to meeting you.

    (*They shake hands.*)

    a. How are you today?   b. How do you do?

POWERS: _____ Mr. Myers. You've come a very long way on this trip, so I hope things are going well. Welcome to San Francisco!

    a. It's nice to meet you . . .   b. I'm doing fine . . .

Variation 2: Looking for Someone

Mr. Malone asks Mrs. Powers to meet Bob Myers at his hotel. They are taking him out to lunch at a restaurant. Mrs. Powers looks for Bob Myers.

Try to complete the following dialog. Then listen and write in the exact words.

POWERS: Mr. Myers?

    X: _____?

POWERS: _____ Mr. Myers from

    Dover Limited?

    X: No, _____. _____

    _____ ask reception to page him?

POWERS: Oh, thank you. I'll do that. _____

    _____.

    X: Oh, _____.

Practice role playing Variation 1 and Variation 2.
Use your real name, but take the position of the characters
in the story.

A Business Lunch

A. Discussion Questions

1. Why do you think industrial robots are important for the new factory?
2. Is it usual in your country to do business over lunch or dinner? Do you think it's a good idea?

B. Story Update

1. What is the purpose of this business lunch?
2. What does Mike Epstein think of Yamashita's robots?
3. What does Shirley Graham think of them?

Now listen to the story update to check your answers.

C.   Pre-Listening

Before you listen to the dialog, answer the following questions.

1.   Who do you think will be the host at the restaurant?

(*Rank your choices from 1–3.*)

   a.   Epstein
   b.   Graham
   c.   Blake

Why do you think so?

2.   Which of the following problems are most important to discuss at the meeting?

(*Rank your choices from 1–4.*)

   a.   spare parts and maintenance in the United States   c.   contract details
   b.   cost of the robots   d.   shipping costs

3.   What do you think is the most likely solution to the problem of maintenance and spare parts?

(*Rank your choices from 1–4.*)

   a.   Yamashita will open an office in the United States.
   b.   Yamashita will ask Advanced Technologies to store extra spare parts.
   c.   Yamashita will train Advanced Technologies' engineers.
   d.   other (why?)

4.   Do you think a final decision will be made at this meeting? Why/Why not?

D.   General Comprehension

Listen to the dialog and mark your answers true (T) or false (F).

1.   There are no major problems.   T   F
2.   Shirley Graham needs more information.   T   F
3.   Advanced Technologies will definitely buy the robots.   T   F
4.   Graham is still worried about doing business with a Japanese company.   T   F
5.   Charles Blake is going to fax his report to Tokyo.   T   F

E.   Detailed Listening

Read the sentences below. Listen to the dialog again and complete the sentences.

1.   EPSTEIN   That was a _____ meal.

      GRAHAM: It was _____.

2. Graham and Blake agree that the basic problem is that Yamashita doesn't have

_____ or _____ in the United States.

3. Blake's first proposal was that
   a. Yamashita open an office in the United States.
   b. Advanced Technologies use their warehouse to store spare parts.
   c. Advanced Technologies take care of maintenance.

4. Graham needs to know a lot more detail before she can make a decision about Blake's

   proposal. Warehouse space is limited, so she needs to know the _____ and the

   _____ of the spare parts.

5. Another reason Graham may decide not to buy from Yamashita is that Advanced

   Technologies has never _____ with a Japanese company before.

F. Functional Phrases 1

1. *Study the table.*

OFFERING	Would (you) like (some more coffee)?
ACCEPTING	That would be very nice. Thank you. Yes, I'd like (a little bit more), please.
REFUSING	Not for me. No, thank you.
REQUESTING	Could we (have some more coffee), please?

2. *In this episode, who* a. *offers?* b. *accepts?* c. *refuses?* d. *requests?*

3. *Try to complete the dialog with phrases from the table above. Then listen and check your answers.*

EPSTEIN: Well, that was a pretty good meal.

GRAHAM: Um, it was delicious.

EPSTEIN: _____ some . . . some more coffee? Shirley?

GRAHAM: _____ No, thank you.

BLAKE: Yes. _____ a little bit more please.

EPSTEIN: Okay. There's the waiter. Waiter, _____ get another cup of

coffee over here, please. Thank you.

> NOTE: Mike Epstein says "Would *anyone* like some more coffee?"
>
> This is because there are two other people with him.
> He could also say "Would *you* like some more coffee?"
> To one person you use "Would *you* like . . .?"

G.   Role Play

Part A

You are host. You want to make sure
your guest(s) have had enough to eat and drink.

Part B

Accept or refuse your host's offers for
more food/drink.

H.   Functional Phrases 2

Confirming, Clarifying, Qualifying

1. *Check these words in your dictionary if you are not sure what they mean.*

CONFIRM   CLARIFY   QUALIFY

Now fill in the gaps in the sentences below. Use one word for each sentence.

a.   I'm phoning to _____ my reservation for Friday night.

b.   I'm sorry, that last point is not very clear to me. Could I ask you to _____ it?

c.   He says his company will buy our products. However I'd like to _____ that

by saying that we still need government approval.

In business it is particularly important that we understand each other exactly, so it is a good idea
to check that you have understood what the other person has said.

2.   *Listen to the dialog.*

What does Charles Blake say to check that he has understood the situation?

BLAKE: Okay, Ms. Graham, _____

_____

Now your basic problem is that we at Yamashita cannot provide adequate

maintenance or spare parts quickly enough.

3. *Has he understood the situation exactly?*

    GRAHAM: Yes. _____ That's my main concern.

    BLAKE: Okay. Now you've rejected the proposal that we use your warehouse for storage

    space for spare parts.

    GRAHAM: Well, _____ Mr. Blake.

4. *What does Shirley Graham say to make sure he understands?*

    GRAHAM: _____ a little.

5. *Match the sentences below to make three logical dialogs.*
    1. Let me see if I understand you correctly. We will be relocating at the end of the year.
    2. Let me see if I understand you correctly—you're saying we should take on more personnel.
    3. As I understand it, you have reservations about the large amount of investment. Is that right?

        a. Not necessarily. Let me clarify our position. It very much depends on whether training could solve the problem.
        b. Well, let me clarify that. Actually, we would prefer to invest in stages, rather than all at once.
        c. Well, not exactly. Let me clarify that a little. It will only be necessary for certain divisions to do so.

I. Role Play

Work in groups of three. Take turns role playing parts A, B, and C below. The situation is the same as above. Then listen to the dialog again and go on to the next page.

Part A	Part B	Part C
You are in Blake's role. You want to confirm your understanding of all the points made by C. Then make a proposal.	You are in Epstein's role. You want A and C to understand each other. You are the host. Make sure everyone is comfortable.	You are in Graham's role. You are worried about several problems. Explain these problems to A.

Variation: Negotiating

This is part of a meeting between two businessmen, Mr. Davis and Mr. Jones.

Comprehension

Listen and answer the questions.

1. What point of the negotiation have they reached?
2. How many problems are there?
3. What action do they decide to take?

Functional Phrases

Now read the dialog below. Imagine the complete dialog. Then look at the list of phrases. Choose the best answer for each blank. Listen again to check your answers.

DAVIS: _____ there are still problems with the delivery date and the size of the discount, but everything else is okay, is that right?

JONES: Yes. _____ The price is higher than we expected, and we need delivery within six months at the latest.

DAVIS: I see. Well, _____ The delivery date is going to be a problem, but _____ and see if it's possible. _____ again? _____ later this week?

JONES: Okay, but _____ I won't be free except for tomorrow afternoon. _____

DAVIS: No, that'll be fine. How about 3:00?

JONES: Okay, good. I'll see you tomorrow, Mr. Davis.

DAVIS: See you then.

I'm afraid . . .	How about . . .	Can we get together . . .
Is that too early?	To summarize . . .	That's right.
I'll see what I can do.	I'll check . . .	

Now practice role playing the variation.

The Disagreement

A. Discussion Questions

1. What is your impression of Shirley Graham?
2. What do you think the next step will be now that the business lunch is finished?

B. Story Update

Listen to the story update and answer the following questions.

1. What other company is mentioned?
2. What are the reasons for and against buying from this other company?

C. Pre-Listening

Before you listen to the dialog, answer the following questions.

1. What is the deadline for installing the robots in the new factory? Why is this a problem?
2. If Epstein and Graham don't agree, who will make the decision?
3. Below are the notes Graham made during the luncheon meeting with Blake. What do you think Graham will decide?

Shirley Graham Vice-President

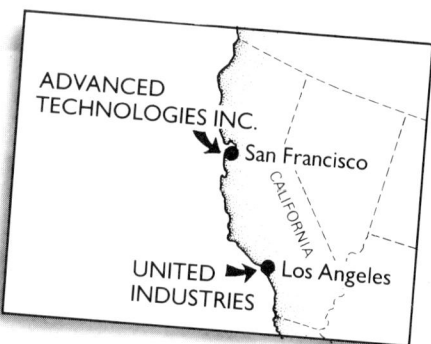

Wed, June 12th
YAMASHITA LTD – BLAKE

Advantages

- Price
- State-of-the-Art Technology
- Excellent maintenance record in Japan

NOTE: United Industries has been a reliable supplier for 15 years.

Disadvantages
- Deadline ??
- No experience in the U.S.
- We have never worked with this company.

D. General Comprehension

Listen to the dialog and mark these sentences true (T) or false (F).

1. Graham wants to buy the robots from United Industries.   T   F
2. Graham is worried about Yamashita's reliability.   T   F
3. Epstein agrees with Graham.   T   F
4. Graham doesn't want to take a risk with Yamashita.   T   F
5. Graham thinks Epstein hasn't done a good job.   T   F

E. Detailed Listening

Now listen to the dialog once more and complete the following sentences.

1. Graham is afraid that

    a. Yamashita's technology is not reliable.
    b. Yamashita cannot be relied on to install the robots on time.
    c. the quality of Yamashita's robots isn't good enough.

2. Graham wants to buy from United Industries because

    a. their robots are less expensive.
    b. she is sure they can install the robots on time.
    c. their technology is just as good as Yamashita's.

3. Epstein says that it is good that Yamashita isn't established in North America, because

    a. his company can get Yamashita's technology first.
    b. Yamashita will design an excellent support system.
    c. Yamashita will discount the price.

4. For Epstein, the main reason to buy from Yamashita is

    a. that the deadline isn't a problem.
    b. that United Industries' robots are too expensive.
    c. that Yamashita's technology is the best.

5. Graham says, "I'm sorry, but I'm afraid on this you're just not going to be able to have it the way you want it." In this conversation, this means

    a. Graham is afraid of Epstein.
    b. she disagrees with Epstein's recommendation.
    c. she is right and he is wrong.

F. Functional Phrases

In this episode Shirley Graham and Mike Epstein both give their opinions and disagree with each other.

1. What do you say when you
    a. agree with someone?
    b. disagree with someone?
    c. give your opinion?

2. *Put the phrases below under the following headings.*

AGREEING	DISAGREEING	GIVING YOUR OPINION

I think (we should) . . .
I agree (with you).
I feel (sure) . . .
You're right.
I'm sorry, but I'm afraid (I can't agree).

3. *Now listen and complete the dialog.*

GRAHAM: . . . Yes, in Japan. The quality of their product is extremely good but I don't know anything about their reliability. Can they be relied on to do this by October 1st? ＿＿＿＿＿＿＿＿＿＿ we've worked with United Industries before and ＿＿＿＿＿＿＿＿＿＿ just go ahead on the deal with them. ＿＿＿＿＿＿＿＿＿＿ they can have everything installed and working by October 1st.

EPSTEIN: Well, look, ＿＿＿＿＿＿＿＿＿＿＿＿＿＿ Shirley, and that is that ＿＿＿＿＿＿＿＿＿＿ they haven't established themselves in the States ＿＿＿＿＿＿＿＿ that's an advantage . . . that's our advantage because we can get their technology before other companies can. If we're willing to take the risk. ＿＿＿＿＿＿＿＿＿＿ take that risk.

GRAHAM: Well, ＿＿＿＿＿＿＿＿ basically that's what it comes down to Mike. You want to take the risk and I really am not willing to. ＿＿＿＿＿＿＿＿＿＿ I can afford to take the risk.

EPSTEIN: Oh, but what have I been doing for the last year? I've been looking for the new technology to really make this factory something special and I think that this is what we need to do. ＿＿＿＿＿＿＿＿ you disagree with this. It's very clear.

GRAHAM: And I think _____

but _____ that there are more disadvantages than advantages.

And _____ on this you're just not going to be able

to have it the way you want it.

4. *Look at the following ways of suggesting a course of action. Which express strong recommendation? Which express more tentative recommendation?*

   a. I really think we have to go ahead with the deal.
   b. We've got to go ahead with the deal.
   c. I think we should go ahead with the deal.
   d. It might be a good idea to go ahead with the deal.
   e. Perhaps we should go ahead with the deal.

5. *How would you feel if someone said the following to you?*

   a. I can't understand why you disagree with this. It's very clear.
   b. I'm sorry but I'm afraid on this you're just not going to be able to have it the way you want it.

   Mike Epstein (a) and Shirley Graham (b) give their opinions in strong language here.

   Can you think of ways of making them sound more polite?

G.   Role Play

Work in pairs. Take turns role playing parts A and B below. The situation is the same as above. Then listen to the dialog again.

Part A

You are in Epstein's role. Try to persuade B that Advanced Technologies should buy robots from Yamashita.

Part B

You are in Graham's role. Explain your reasons for not buying robots from Yamashita. Explain the reasons for buying from United Industries.

Variation: Making a Choice

Here are two parts of a dialog. Read the part on the left (Mr. Malone's part). Now find the correct order for the part on the right (Mrs. Powers' part). After you have finished, listen and check your answers.

Malone

1. I think we should hire John Hart. He has ten years of experience and he's 35 years old, quite mature. What do you think?

2. Yes, he does have an MBA degree, but he doesn't have any real job experience.

3. Yes, that's a good point. Maybe we need more information. Let's talk with them both again.

4. Well, I agree, time is a problem. But this new position is very important. We can wait one more day. Would you mind calling them back?

Now practice role playing the variation.

Powers

a. Do you really think that's necessary? A second interview is a good idea, but I don't think we have the time. I think we really have to decide today.

b. I don't agree. I think we should hire Kevin Ward. He's much better educated, and very bright.

c. That's true, but Mr. Hart has only four years' experience in sales.

d. All right. I'll try to schedule them both for tomorrow afternoon.

Keeping In Touch

A. Story Update

Listen to the story update and answer these questions.

1. Do you think Shirley Graham's decision was a good decision?
   Why (not)?

2. Do you think Shirley Graham is a good manager?
   Why (not)?

3. What do you think of Epstein?

B. Pre-Listening

Before you listen to the dialog, answer the following questions.

1. What will Blake's reaction be to Graham's decision?

    a.   He will be surprised.
    b.   He will not be surprised.

    Why?

2. Epstein is not happy with the decision. Will he:
    a.   tell Blake his opinion.
    b.   not tell Blake his opinion.

    Why?

3. In this business situation, Blake and Epstein should

    a.   arrange to stay in touch.
    b.   not arrange to stay in touch.

    Why?

C. General Comprehension

Listen to the dialog and mark these sentences true (T) or false (F).

1. Blake is surprised by the decision not to buy from Yamashita.   T   F
2. Epstein tells Blake he isn't happy with the decision.   T   F
3. Blake is going to return to Japan immediately.   T   F
4. Epstein invites Blake to play golf with him.   T   F
5. Blake is busy, so he can't accept Epstein's invitation.   T   F

D. Detailed Listening

Now listen once more and complete the following sentences.

1. Blake says this is a valuable experience because

    a.   their robots aren't good enough for the North American market.
    b.   he is under a lot of pressure.
    c.   now he knows what their biggest problem will be.

2. Epstein says that they couldn't convince Graham to buy from Yamashita because

    a.   Graham didn't like the quality of the robots.
    b.   she was under a lot of time pressure.
    c.   she was incompetent.

3. Tomorrow afternoon Blake is flying to New York to

   a. visit friends.

   b. meet with prospective customers.

   c. look for a new job.

4. Epstein wants to stay in touch because

   a. he is interested in Yamashita's robots for possible future projects.

   b. he enjoys playing golf with Blake.

   c. Shirley Graham is going to be fired and he will take over.

5. Epstein has made reservations

   a. at a restaurant.

   b. to play golf at his club.

   c. to fly to New York.

E. Functional Phrases

1. *Below (a–f) you have definitions for the following:*

> EXPRESS DISAPPOINTMENT   REQUEST
> GIVE (AN) OPINION   ACCEPT
> QUALIFY   INVITE

Complete the definitions by inserting the correct words from the box.

a. When you make a _____, you ask someone to do something.

b. When you _____ what you have said, you modify it, showing that you are

taking another point (of view) into consideration.

c. When you _____ your _____, you say what you think.

d. When something you hoped for does not happen, you will probably say something to

_____ your _____.

e. When you _____ an invitation, you say "Yes."

f. When you _____ someone to do something, you ask them if they would like

to do it.

Now match the definitions you just completed to these phrases.

    i.   It's (just) too bad . . .

   ii.   That sounds like a great idea. Sure.

  iii.   It's (just) too bad we couldn't convince Shirley. Still, I understand her point too.

  iv.   I'd like to ask, if you could just keep in touch later.

   v.   Would you like to join me in a game of golf this afternoon?

  vi.   I think that your machinery is still the best on the market.

2.   *Listen to the dialog line by line and write the exact words.*

EPSTEIN: Well, _____ but _____ things worked

out the way we thought they might.

BLAKE: Yeah, but this has been a valuable experience for us. Now we know what our

biggest problem will be with the North American market.

EPSTEIN: Well for me, of course, I'm still not happy. _____ your

machinery is the best on the market. _____ that I . . . we

couldn't convince Shirley. _ _____, I can understand her point too. She's

under a lot of pressure here to get this . . . this new operation going by October.

BLAKE: Sure.

     . . . .

EPSTEIN: Also, _____,

keep in touch later. I'm very interested to know what happens. In the future, you

know, we never know what's going to happen but it may be possible for us to

work together.

BLAKE: Okay, _____ Mike.

EPSTEIN: One other thing. _____ this afternoon?

BLAKE: Well, I have no plans.

EPSTEIN: Well, I remember the nice game of golf that we had together when I was in

Tokyo. I have a membership in a golf club just across the Bay here and I've

made some reservations. _____

in a round of golf this afternoon?

BLAKE: _____ Sure.

F. Role Play

Work in pairs. Take turns role playing parts A and B below. The situation is the same as on p. 50. Then listen to the dialog again.

Part A

You are in Epstein's role. Tell B that your company has decided not to buy robots from Yamashita. Try to keep a good relationship with B and invite B to join you in a game of golf.

Part B

You are in Blake's role. Explain why you think Shirley Graham decided not to buy from you. Try to keep a good relationship with A. You are going to fly to New York tomorrow.

Variation: Making a Polite Refusal

Ms. Cinthia Winthrop and Mr. Robert Vale have just finished a business meeting. Ms. Winthrop is a sales executive for a New York company. Mr. Vale is on a business trip from London, and he is not interested in doing business with her.

Comprehension

Listen to the dialog and answer the following questions.

1. What does Ms. Winthrop invite Mr. Vale to do?
2. How does Mr. Vale refuse both invitations?
3. Do you think they will keep in touch? Why?

Functional Phrases

Now listen again. Then look at the dialog below and fill in the blanks using the phrases from the list **below**. *Note that the phrases in the list below are different from the ones in the dialog. Choose the phrase which has the closest meaning to what you hear.*

WINTHROP: _____ to see our factory while you are in New York?

VALE: That's very kind of you. _____ my schedule is booked up all next week.

WINTHROP: _____ Well, _____ I may be in London early next year and . . .

VALE: Okay. Please give me a call.

WINTHROP: Thank you. _____ Well, it's nearly 12:30. _____ for lunch?

VALE: _____ I have other plans. _____

WINTHROP: _____ Perhaps another time.

I'm sorry to hear that.	Unfortunately . . .	I certainly will.
Would you like . . .	I'd like to keep in touch.	I appreciate the invitation.
My pleasure.	I'm afraid I'm not.	Are you free . . .?

Now practice role playing the variation.

New Customer

A. Story Update

Listen to the story update.

1. Where is Charles Blake now?
2. Who is Mr. Chapman?
3. Which company is interested in Yamashita's robots? Why?

B. Pre-Listening

Before you listen to the dialog, answer the following questions.

1. According to the following letter, when is Mr. Blake scheduled to meet Mr. Chapman?

> Stewart R. Chapman
> Vice-President, Engineering
> Federal Motors Building
> New York, NY 10016
> U.S.A.
>
> Dear Mr. Chapman
>
> Thank you for your letter of May 20th. I am looking forward to
> meeting you, and am pleased that you can meet with me the week of
> June 17 while I am in New York. I will call your office on Friday
> morning, June 14 to confirm the exact time and details.
>
> As you requested, I have enclosed the latest information on our
> industrial robots. I am confident that our robots will meet your
> highest standards, and I look forward to discussing the details.
> If things work out, I hope to meet you here in Tokyo in the not too
> distant future.
>
> Sincerely,
>
> *Charles Blake*
>
> Charles Blake
> Manager, International Sales

2. In the above letter, a business meeting is being arranged. In your opinion, what are good reasons for changing or breaking a business appointment?

    (Rank your choices from 1 – 5.)

    a.   a busy schedule with more important matters/clients
    b.   personal matters (e.g. illness, family problems, etc.)
    c.   transportation/weather difficulties
    d.   forgetting the appointment
    e.   other (give examples)
    Why?

C. General Comprehension

Listen to the dialog and mark these sentences true (T) or false (F).

1. Dave Gomez and Charles Blake have met before. T F
2. Gomez apologizes to Blake. T F
3. Mr. Chapman is busy, so they have to wait. T F
4. Blake will meet with Gomez instead of Chapman. T F
5. Gomez wants to talk business immediately. T F

D. Detailed Listening

Now listen to the dialog once more and complete the following sentences.

1. Blake has an appointment with

    a. Mr. Chapman later this week.
    b. Mr. Chapman at 10:30.
    c. Mr. Gomez at 10:30.

2. Mr. Gomez explains that Mr. Chapman

    a. is out of town on company business.
    b. has quit working for Federal Motors.
    c. is out of town on a personal matter.

3. Mr. Chapman will

    a. meet with Blake as soon as he returns.
    b. not be involved in the negotiations.
    c. be out of town for several weeks.

4. Mr. Gomez knows about

    a. Yamashita, but not its products.
    b. Yamashita and its products.
    c. industrial robots, but not Yamashita.

5. Mr. Gomez suggests that they

    a. wait for Chapman to return.
    b. get to know each other a bit before discussing business.
    c. reschedule the meeting for later this afternoon.

E. Functional Phrases

Introducing, Greeting

1. *Which of the phrases below do you use*

    — on the phone?
    — in face-to-face contact?
    — both?

a. This is (your name)	h. May I have your name, please?
b. My name is . . .	i. Who's calling, please?
c. I'm (your name)	j. Mr. Chapman, I have a
d. The name is . . .	Mr. Blake on the line for you.
e. I have an appointment to see	k. There's a Mr. Blake here for you,
Mr. Chapman.	Mr. Chapman.
f. I'd like to speak with	l. Welcome to . . .
Mr. Chapman.	m. Pleased to meet you.
g. Can I help you?	

2. *Complete this dialog using some of the phrases above. Then listen and check your answers.*

RECEPTIONIST: Good morning sir, _____?

BLAKE: Yeah, _____ to see Mr. Chapman,

Stewart Chapman at 10:30.

RECEPTIONIST: Oh, Mr. Chapman. _____?

BLAKE: Yeah, _____ is Blake, Charles Blake of Yamashita

Limited.

RECEPTIONIST: All right, thank you. Just a moment please . . .

. . . . . .

GOMEZ: Good morning Mr. Blake. _____ Federal Motors. My

name is Dave Gomez.

BLAKE: _____ Mr. Gomez.

GOMEZ: Nice to meet you, sir. Did you have a good trip to New York?

BLAKE: Yeah, and I'm looking forward to staying here for a few days and doing some

business.

3. *Why does Dave Gomez address Charles Blake as "sir"?*

Requesting, Suggesting, Accepting, Apologizing

4. *Look at the sentences below. In which is the speaker very confident, in which is he less confident?*

    a. I'd like to work with you on this, if I may.
    b. I'd like to work with you on this.
    c. Could we possibly work together on this?
    d. I'd like to work with you on this, if that would be all right.
    e. Why don't we go into the office and sit down and relax for a few minutes and we can get some coffee or tea if you'd like?
    f. Let's go into the office and sit down and relax for a few minutes and get some coffee or tea.

    Which do you think Dave Gomez says?

5. *Listen to the dialog and complete the sentences.*

    GOMEZ: Great. Uh, Mr. Chapman asked me to apologize to you. He was called out of town on a personal matter very suddenly. And he does assure me he is looking forward to meeting with you when he gets back.

    BLAKE: Uh-huh.

    GOMEZ: In the meantime, I'm quite familiar with Yamashita and your products, and so
    _____ work with you _____
    _____?

    BLAKE: Okay, sure. And _____ about Mr. Chapman's absence.
    _____

    GOMEZ: Great. Uh, you must be tired from your trip. _____ go into the office and sit down and relax for a few minutes and we can get some coffee or tea _____?

    BLAKE: Okay, that sounds great.

    GOMEZ: Great.

6. *How do you think Charles Blake feels when he hears Mr. Chapman is out of town? What does he say? Is this a good response?*

F.   Role Play

Part A	Part B	Part C
You are in Dave Gomez's role. Explain why Mr. Chapman is absent and introduce yourself to C. Make C feel comfortable. Explain that you will act in Mr. Chapman's place.	You are the receptionist at Federal Motors.	You are in Blake's role. You have an appointment with Mr. Stewart Chapman. Find out why Mr. Chapman is absent.

Variation: Asking a Favor

Sandra Powers calls Bill Malone at home on Sunday.
Imagine the complete conversation.
Then listen to the dialog and write the exact words.

MALONE: _____.

POWERS: Hello, Bill. Sorry to call you at home.

MALONE: _____?

POWERS: I'm afraid I've got a problem. My mother is quite ill and I have to fly to Miami today.

I hate to ask, but would you mind meeting Bob Myers of Dover Limited, tomorrow?

MALONE: _____

_____

_____?

POWERS: He'll be there at 10:30.

MALONE: _____.

POWERS: Thanks! Again, I'd like to apologize for this inconvenience.

MALONE: _____

_____

_____.

POWERS: Thank you. I hope I can be back by Wednesday, but I'm just not sure right now.

MALONE: _____.

POWERS: Thanks again. I appreciate it. I'll call you tomorrow afternoon around 4:00.

MALONE: _____.

Now practice role playing the variation.

Negotiations

A. Story Update

Look at Charles Blake's diary entries.
Listen to the story update.

Which entries are incorrect?

	JUNE
Tuesday 18th	Meeting at Federal Motors - technology, price, how used in Japan
Wednesday 19th	Meeting with Gomez to discuss outstanding problems Call Advanced Technologies
Thursday 20th	Chapman returns to N.Y.
Friday 21st	Golf with Chapman and Gomez

B. Discussion Questions

1. What problems do you think might be discussed at today's meeting?
2. What kind of language problems do you think might be important to discuss?

C. Pre-Listening

Before you listen to the dialog, answer the following questions.

1. What do you think are Yamashita's main strengths?

    (Rank your choices from 1–4.)

    a. aftersales service
    b. price
    c. quality and high performance
    d. good reputation

2. What are some important differences between international sales/service and domestic sales/service for a product such as industrial robots? Which of these differences are problems that are often difficult to solve?

3. How much time is usually necessary to solve these kinds of problems for an important new customer?

    (Rank your choices from 1–4.)

    a. six weeks or less
    b. three months
    c. six months
    d. approximately one year

4. Do you think Federal Motors will buy Yamashita's robots?

D. General Comprehension

Listen to the dialog and mark these sentences true (T) or false (F).

1. Time pressure is a major problem.   T   F
2. Yamashita has already translated the service manual into English.   T   F
3. Gomez needs more information about Yamashita's performance record in Japan.   T   F
4. Gomez isn't satisfied with Blake's answers.   T   F
5. From Blake's point of view, this meeting is successful.   T   F

E. Detailed Listening

Listen to the dialog again. Indicate the correct answer by circling a, b, or c.

1. Gomez needs a group of technical advisors

    a. to translate the service manual into English.
    b. to train his engineers and workers.
    c. to provide language training.

2. The technical advisors can come to Federal Motors from Japan

    a. as soon as they learn to speak English.
    b. within a few months.
    c. anytime they are needed.

3. Blake says the service manual will be ready

    a. in two weeks at the most.
    b. in a short time, but he's got to check.
    c. in several months.

4. Gomez needs the service manual in English

    a. in two to three weeks.
    b. in a month or two.
    c. anytime before January 1st.

5. Blake will send performance reports of the robots to Gomez

    a. early next year.
    b. as soon as they are finished.
    c. shortly after he gets back to Tokyo.

6. Make a list of the points raised by Dave Gomez and the solutions offered by Charles Blake.

F. Functional Phrases

1. *Match each phrase in Column A with a phrase from Column B that has a similar meaning.*

	A		B
a.	As I told you . . .	i.	I'll do it.
b.	Could you give me . . .?	ii.	I don't think we will have any difficulty with that.
c.	I'd have to get back to you.	iii.	That seems fine.
d.	That sounds quite reasonable.	iv.	I'd like to have . . .
e.	Why don't I . . .?	v.	Is that all?
f.	That shouldn't be a problem.	vi.	I could . . .
g.	I'll see to it.	vii.	As I mentioned before . . .
h.	Is there anything else?	viii.	I'd have to check that and then let you know.

2. *Complete the dialog with a phrase from Column A. Then listen to the dialog to check your answers.*

    GOMEZ: Great, great, that sounds good. Another one of our major concerns is the service manual. We're quite concerned about getting a service manual in English that will be easy to read and very clear and useful for our engineers.

BLAKE: Yeah. Again, _____ we are preparing a translation of the
Japanese manual we have now, and we expect that to be ready in a short time.

GOMEZ: By a short time . . . _____ an estimate?

BLAKE: Uh, I'd like to say two weeks, _____
but probably about two or three weeks.

GOMEZ: _____
As you know we have until January 1st to actually install these machines and get them
operating, so we're under no deadline pressure here.

BLAKE: Okay, well that gives us a fair amount of time to work with.

GOMEZ: Plenty of time. That sounds good, Mr. Blake. Uh, another concern is your
professional record—uh—performance record in Japan with these machines.

BLAKE: _____ send you some reports that we have on the
performance of the robot in some Japanese companies who are also our clients.
And I'm sure you'll be quite pleased with what you see.

GOMEZ: Okay, great. Could you get those off to me within a few weeks?

BLAKE: Sure. _____.
In fact, as soon as I get back to Tokyo _____.

GOMEZ: Excellent. Uh, thank you very much.

BLAKE: _____.

GOMEZ: Well, no. That covers all the major points.

BLAKE: Okay. Fine.

GOMEZ: Sounds good . . .

G. Role Play

*Work in pairs. Take turns role playing parts A and B below. The situation is the same as above.
Then listen to the dialog again and go on to the next exercise.*

Part A

You are in Gomez's role. Summarize
all problem areas and confirm your
understanding of B's proposals.

Part B

You are in Blake's role. Confirm your
understanding of all problem areas and
propose solutions.

Variation 1: Telling someone there have been changes

How do you think this story ends?

1. *Listen to the dialog and answer these questions.*

   a. What happened to Shirley Graham?
   b. Why is Mike Epstein calling?
   c. Why isn't Charles Blake's office in Tokyo open?

2. *Look at the dialog. Imagine you are Charles Blake.*

   What do you say? (You do not have to remember his exact words.)

   Now listen to the dialog and write in the exact words.

Charles Blake	**Mike Epstein**
1. _____ _____	Charles. This is Mike Epstein.
2. _____ _____	Well, that's why I'm calling you. There have been some changes here, and I wanted to let you know.
3. _____	Well, Shirley Graham has resigned, and I've been put in charge of our project.
4. _____ _____ _____	Thank you. But that's not all. I'm still interested in getting your machines for our new factory, and I've been able to extend the deadline for a month, to November 1st. Do you think you can make it?
5. _____ _____ _____	When are you flying back to Tokyo?
6. _____	Could you change your flight and stop by here for a day or two?
7. _____ _____ _____	If you could call me back within a couple of hours and let me know, I'd appreciate it.

8. _____   Right. I forgot about the time difference
   _____   . . .
   _____

Variation 2

Here is an alternative ending.

First put the dialog in order. Then listen to the dialog to check your answer.

Blake

a. Well we just finished our meeting, and things look very good. They like our technology, and there are no serious problems. Some of their people will fly to Tokyo the week after next, and if things work out, I'm pretty sure we'll get our first big order in North America. I'm very pleased.

b. Thanks for calling, and good luck with your new job.

f. Well, that's great news. I'll be looking forward to hearing from you.

i. Yes? This is Charles Blake speaking.

k. Sounds good Mike. And maybe we'll even get in a round of golf.

l. I'll certainly do that.

n. Oh, Mike, it's good to hear from you. What's up?

o. Well, congratulations.

Epstein

c. Well, congratulations. Next time we get together, we'll have to celebrate.

d. If you could keep me informed of any new developments, I'd really appreciate it.

e. How did things go in New York?

g. Thanks. But the reason I'm calling you is that I'll be working on a project very similar to the one I was working on before, and there's a good chance that we'll be interested in your machines.

h. Well, to begin with, I've decided to leave Advanced Technologies and join another company. I've been thinking about it for quite a while now, and last week I was offered a position at Data Systems Inc.

j. Good idea. Well, have a good trip back to Tokyo, Charles.

m. Hello Charles. This is Mike Epstein calling.

p. Thanks.

Now practice role playing the variations.

FUNCTIONING IN BUSINESS
NEW EDITION
Answer Key and Transcripts

INTRODUCTION

Part 1

COMPANY **Yamashita Ltd.**	**Advanced Technologies**
HEAD OFFICE **Tokyo**	**San Francisco**
PRODUCT(S) **Industrial equipment, robots**	**Electronic equipment, office computers**
MAIN MARKET **Japan**	**U.S.**
SECONDARY MARKET **—**	**Overseas and Canada**

Transcript

This is the story of an important business trip. It begins with two companies, Yamashita Limited and Advanced Technologies. The main characters of this story are Charles Blake and Mike Epstein.

My name is Charles Blake. I work for a Japanese company, Yamashita Limited. Our head office is in Tokyo, Japan. We manufacture industrial equipment and robots. At this time 100 per cent of our sales of industrial robots is in Japan.

Hi, I'm Mike Epstein. I work for Advanced Technologies, an American company. Our head office is in San Francisco, California. We manufacture electronic components and office computers. Eighty per cent of our sales are in the U.S., and twenty per cent are overseas and in Canada.

Part 2

1. CHARLES BLAKE   a. **F**   b. **F**   c. **T**   · d. **T**
    MIKE EPSTEIN   a. **T**   b. **T**   c. **F**   d. **F**

2. See transcript below.

Transcript

Charles Blake

I graduated from Columbia University in 1971. I studied international relations and a little Japanese. After graduation I worked for a small import-export company in New York. I was with their salesforce for about five years. Then, in 1976, I began working for Yamashita, a Japanese company. I am currently with their head office in Tokyo. **My responsibility is to begin the export of industrial robots to North America.** I live in Tokyo and I'm married to a Japanese woman. We have a child, a son. I enjoy playing golf and tennis, but I'm afraid I don't have a lot of spare time.

Mike Epstein

I graduated from Stanford University in 1973. I studied electrical engineering. After graduation I went to work for a company in San Francisco for two years. Then in 1976 I went back to school and I got my MBA. In 1978 I went to work for Advanced Technologies Incorporated. I'm now a systems engineer. **It's my responsibility to help cut the production costs for a new factory that's going to be built near San Francisco.** I want to increase the use of industrial robots to cut costs and improve productivity. I am divorced and I have no children. I enjoy playing golf, when I have the time.

Part 3

2. a. **F**   b. **F**   c. **T**   d. **F**   e. **T**   f. **F**

Transcript

The story
The story began two months ago in April. Here is more information about the story.

Two months ago, in April, Mike Epstein of Advanced Technologies went to Tokyo, Japan. He attended a trade show and saw many industrial robots. At the trade show he was very interested in the industrial robots made by Yamashita Limited. Then he met Charles Blake of Yamashita Limited and they talked about Yamashita's robots. After the trade show, Mr. Epstein and Mr. Blake played golf together and then Mr. Epstein returned to the U.S.

Last month, in May, Mr. Blake of Yamashita Ltd., wrote a letter to Mr. Epstein. He said he would be in the U.S. in June, from June 10th through June 20th. If possible, he wanted to meet with Mr. Epstein.

Mr. Epstein wrote back and invited him to come to Advanced Technologies in San Francisco. Mr. Epstein wants to meet with Mr. Blake several times between June 11th and June 14th. Mr. Epstein is very interested in buying Yamashita's robots.

This is the end of the Introductory Unit.

EPISODE 1   Checking In

A.   Story Update

Transcript

It is Monday, June 10th. Mr. Blake, from Yamashita Ltd., is in San Francisco. He wants to meet with Mr. Epstein of Advanced Technologies. Mr. Blake arrived in San Francisco this afternoon on a flight from Tokyo, Japan. He is now checking in to the Embassy Suites Hotel in Silicon Valley which is south of San Francisco. It is four-fifteen in the afternoon.

C.   General Comprehension

1. **T**   2. **F**   3. **F**   4. **F**   5. **F**   6. **F**

D.   Detailed Listening

> NAME   **Charles Blake**
> RESERVATION NUMBER   **14689**
> DATE OF ARRIVAL   **6/10/9**..
> ROOM NUMBER   **685**
> PRICE OF ROOM   **$120**
> METHOD OF PAYMENT   **Cash** / Credit Card*
>   Credit card details: **American Express**

E.   Functional Phrases

2. a. **ii.; v.**   b. **i.; ii.**   c. **vii.**   d. **iv.**   e. **iii.**   f. **vi.**

3. and 4.   Check your answers by looking at the transcript.

Transcript

CLERK: Good evening, sir. Welcome to the Embassy Suites Hotel. **Can I help you?**
BLAKE: Yeah, my name is Blake, Charles Blake. I have a confirmed reservation.

CLERK:	Mr. Blake, Yes. And the reservation number?
BLAKE:	Let's see. Er, here it is—14689.
CLERK:	14689. Let me check. Yes, sir, we have your reservation right here. That's for June 10th through the 13th, Monday through Thursday night. **Is that correct**, sir?
BLAKE:	**Yes, that's fine.**
CLERK:	Okay, and the room sir is 685 on the sixth floor. I've got the key right here and I'll get a bellman for you right away.
BLAKE:	Okay. What was the price of the room again?
CLERK:	That room is $120 a night.
BLAKE:	Okay, fine. **Can I** use my American Express card for that?
CLERK:	**Yes, certainly**, sir. **Can I make a** print of your card before we check you in?
BLAKE:	Sure, there you are.
CLERK:	Okay, thank you. All right, fine. We're all set here Mr. Blake, and I'll get the bellman right away. We'll get you to your room.
BLAKE:	Oh, by the way, there's a chance I will be staying one more day, so I might be leaving on Saturday. Is that okay?
CLERK:	Let me check. Well sir, **I'm afraid** we're all booked up for Friday night, but something may open up. Can I let you know?
BLAKE:	Okay, **if you could** let me know as soon as possible, **I would appreciate it.**
CLERK:	Yes, we can do that for you, sir. Okay, and here's your key, sir. I'll get the bellman. Bellman, front!

Variation: Cashing a Check

Comprehension

1. **Yes**   2. **No**   3. **No**   4. **Yes**

Functional Phrases/Transcript

BANK TELLER:	**May I help you?**
CUSTOMER:	Yes. **Can I** change British pounds for American dollars here?
BANK TELLER:	Yes, certainly, sir. How much would you like to change?
CUSTOMER:	One hundred pounds please. Also, **could I** cash this personal check from my London Bank?
BANK TELLER:	**I'm afraid** that isn't possible. Our policy is that we do not cash out of town checks.
CUSTOMER:	It's very important that I cash this check . . .
BANK TELLER:	Yes, I understand, but the bank policy . . .
CUSTOMER:	**Could I** see the manager please?
BANK TELLER:	**I'm sorry but** the manager, Mr. Grover, is out right now. The Assistant Manager, Ms. Grace is in. Would that be all right?
CUSTOMER:	**Yes. That's fine.** Thank you.
BANK TELLER:	Certainly. One moment please.

EPISODE 2   Making an Appointment

A.   Story Update

Transcript

Mr. Blake is now at the Embassy Suites Hotel, south of San Francisco, in Silicon Valley. He checked in to the hotel a few minutes ago. Now he wants to make an appointment with Mr. Mike Epstein, of Advanced Technologies. He wants to make the appointment for tomorrow, Tuesday, June 11th. Mr. Epstein knows Blake's schedule and is expecting his call.

C. General Comprehension

1 b; 2 b; 3 b.

D. Detailed Listening

Transcript

Tuesday June 11th	Wednesday June 12th
Mike Epstein - 11.15 hotel → lunch and look around S.F.	Lunch - Shirley Graham Vice-President of A.T. ?

RECEPTIONIST:	Advanced Technologies. **May I help you?**
BLAKE:	Yes. **This is** Charles Blake from Yamashita Limited **and I'd like to speak with** Mike Epstein, please.
RECEPTIONIST:	Just a minute and I'll put you through.
EPSTEIN:	Epstein.
RECEPTIONIST:	Mr. Epstein, I have a Mr. Blake from Yamashita on the line.
EPSTEIN:	Okay. Thanks. Mr. Blake.
BLAKE:	Hello, Mr. Epstein. **How are you?**
EPSTEIN:	**I'm fine thanks.** How are you?
BLAKE:	Great. I had a nice flight and it was on time.
EPSTEIN:	When did you get into San Francisco?
BLAKE:	I just arrived a few moments ago.
EPSTEIN:	**Say, when shall we get together?**
BLAKE:	Well, I was hoping that we could perhaps arrange a meeting for tomorrow sometime.
EPSTEIN:	Uh, I'll tell you what. I'm free after eleven o'clock. **How's that sound?**
BLAKE:	That sounds fine with me.
EPSTEIN:	Okay. Uh, where are you staying?
BLAKE:	I'm staying at the Embassy Suites. It's about twenty minutes south of the airport.
EPSTEIN:	Uh, that's real close to my office here. I'll tell you what, uh, I'll meet you tomorrow around 11.15. Then we can go to lunch and then I'll show you around San Francisco.
BLAKE:	That sounds very nice.
EPSTEIN:	Great. Uh, just **one other thing** . . . I would like to introduce you to one of our Vice-Presidents, Ms. Shirley Graham. Now she's the manager of the project that I'm working on and I was wondering if we could get together again, **say** Wednesday?
BLAKE:	Ah-h, I have no plans on Wednesday, and I would like to meet her.
EPSTEIN:	Okay, uh, if you could keep your schedule free uh around lunchtime on Wednesday and then I'll finalize that appointment with her.
BLAKE:	Okay, very good.
EPSTEIN:	All right. I'll look forward to seeing you tomorrow morning.
BLAKE:	Okay. **That's tomorrow, 11:15 at the hotel.**
EPSTEIN:	Yes, okay.
BLAKE:	I'm looking forward to seeing you too.
EPSTEIN:	Okay, see you then.
BLAKE:	Bye-bye.
EPSTEIN:	Bye-bye.

4

E. Functional Phrases

See the transcript for answers 2. and 3., 5., 6., 7., and 8.
4. a.

Variations: Making an Appointment; Leaving a Message

Variation 1: Answers/Transcript

a., a., b., a.

BLISS:	Webber Industries, may I help you?
MILTON:	Yes. **This is Roberta Milton.**
BLISS:	This is Sam Bliss speaking. How are you Ms. Milton?
MILTON:	**Fine and you?**
BLISS:	Just fine, thank you.
MILTON:	I'm calling to see if we can arrange a meeting. There are several matters I'd like to discuss with you.
BLISS:	Okay, when would be convenient?
MILTON:	**Could we meet tomorrow?**
BLISS:	Yes, that's possible. What time would be convenient?
MILTON:	**How about 2:30?**
BLISS:	Fine. I'm looking forward to seeing you.
MILTON:	Me too. Okay, in your office at 2:30 tomorrow, right?
BLISS:	Right. See you then.
MILTON:	See you tomorrow.

Variation 2: Transcript

RECEPTIONIST:	Webber Industries, **can I help you?**
MILTON:	**Yes. This is Roberta Milton** from Myer's Shipping Company. **Could I speak with Mr. Webber, please?**
RECEPTIONIST:	**I'm afraid** Mr. Webber is not here right now. Can I take a message?
MILTON:	Yes. Could you please ask Mr. Webber to call me back before 5:00 today?
RECEPTIONIST:	Yes, of course. **Would you please spell your last name?**
MILTON:	Certainly. M-I-L-T-O-N.
RECEPTIONIST:	**Could I have your telephone number please?**
MILTON:	Yes. 877-3088.

EPISODE 3   Confirming Plans

A. Story Update

Transcript

It is now Tuesday, June 11th. It is four o'clock in the afternoon. Mr. Epstein, from Advanced Technologies, met with Mr. Blake, from Yamashita Ltd., earlier today. They had lunch together and talked about industrial robots. Mr. Blake wants to sell his company's industrial robots to Advanced Technologies, Mr. Epstein's company.

   Mr. Epstein's boss is Ms. Shirley Graham. She is in charge of a large project to build a new factory. The new factory is scheduled for completion this October. Tomorrow she is going to meet with Mr. Epstein and Mr. Blake. Mr. Epstein needs to confirm the arrangements with her. He is now at her office.

C. General Comprehension

1. F   2. F   3. T   4. F   5. T

D. Detailed Listening

1. **b.**   2. **a.**   3. **b.**   4. **b.**   5. **c.**

E. Functional Phrases

2., and 4. Check your answers by looking at the transcript.

Functional Phrases/Transcript

GRAHAM: Come in.

EPSTEIN: Oh, Shirley, **do you have a minute?**

GRAHAM: Sure. Come on in Mike. **Have a seat.**

EPSTEIN: Oh, thanks. Listen, I just wanted to let you know that I've made reservations for lunch tomorrow afternoon at 12:15. Okay?

GRAHAM: With Mr. Blake?

EPSTEIN: **That's right**, of Yamashita Limited.

GRAHAM: Okay. So, we should leave here at . . .?

EPSTEIN: About 12:00.

GRAHAM: 12:00 **sounds just fine.**

EPSTEIN: I'll pick you up here at 12 o'clock and we can go to his hotel together.

GRAHAM: All right.

EPSTEIN: Okay.

GRAHAM: Now, have you already discussed any of the project with him?

EPSTEIN: Yes, I did. I had an excellent meeting with him this afternoon.

GRAHAM: And did you tell him that my main concerns are this October deadline and also the fact that they have no aftersales service in the States?

EPSTEIN: Yes, I did and again I was very impressed with his flexibility and his . . . **I think** that we can work things out with him.

GRAHAM: Okay. As long as it's clear to both of you that it has to be worked out, and before October, because that's our deadline.

EPSTEIN: Well, again, **I understand your reservations** Shirley, but again the technology of their product is really excellent. I think we really have to go ahead with this.

GRAHAM: Yes. All right. Well, **let's discuss it further tomorrow.** All right?

EPSTEIN: Okay. All right. Thank you. We'll see you tomorrow.

GRAHAM: We'll see you around 12:00.

EPSTEIN: Okay.

3. **b.**

DISAGREEING POLITELY	GIVING AN OPINION	STALLING
I can see why you don't agree with what I'm saying, but . . . I understand your reservations, but . . .	I think . . . In my opinion . . .	Let's discuss it further tomorrow. I don't think that this is the best time to talk about it.

Variations: Checking an Appointment; Changing an Appointment

Variation 1: Answers/Transcript

1. **e.**   2. **c.**   3. **a.**   4. **b.**   5. **d.**

POWERS: Excuse me. Do you have a minute?

MALONE: Certainly. Please come in.

POWERS: Thanks. I made an appointment for us to see Mr. Myers. Are you still free at 11:00 on Wednesday?

MALONE: 11:00 on Wednesday? I'm afraid not. I'm busy all morning.

POWERS: That's too bad.

MALONE: How about 1:00 on Friday?

POWERS: That's fine with me.
MALONE: Would you call him back and see if Friday is good for him?
POWERS: Sure. I'll call him right away.

Variation 2: Answers/Transcript

1. b., b., a., b., a., b.

MYERS: Hello. **This is** Bob Myers speaking.
POWERS: Hello. This is Sandra Powers from Delta Electronics. **I'm sorry** but Mr. Malone is busy on Wednesday. If it's **convenient** for you, could we change our appointment to 1:00 on Friday?
MYERS: **I understand** that you're very busy, but Friday is too late. We have some very serious problems. **I think** we should meet as soon as possible.
POWERS: I see. **Could** I call you back later today? I want to check our schedule for Thursday.
MYERS: Good. I'll be expecting your call later today.

EPISODE 4   An Important Introduction

A. Story Update

Transcript

It is now Wednesday, June 12th. Yesterday Mr. Charles Blake from Yamashita Ltd. and Mr. Mike Epstein from Advanced Technologies met for lunch. After their meeting, Mr. Epstein took Mr. Blake on a short tour of San Francisco.

Today, Mr. Blake is going to meet Ms. Graham. Ms. Graham is a Vice-President at Advanced Technologies. She is in charge of a large project to build a new factory. Mr. Blake wants to sell his company's industrial robots for use in the new factory. Ms. Graham is interested in Yamashita's robots. However, she is also worried about several problems, such as aftersales service, spare parts, and storage space. She is also worried about doing business with a foreign company such as Yamashita Ltd.

Mike Epstein and Shirley Graham have arrived at the Embassy Suites Hotel and are looking for Charles Blake. They are scheduled to meet him and to have lunch together.

C. General Comprehension

1. F   2. F   3. T   4. F

D. Detailed Listening

1. a.   2. b.   3. b.   4. b.   5. a.

E. Functional Phrases

2. and 5. Check your answers by looking at the transcript.

EPSTEIN: Now, let's see. Where is he? Oh, there he is over there reading the newspaper.
GRAHAM: Ah.
EPSTEIN: Mr. Blake!
BLAKE: Oh, hi, Mike. **How are you** today?
EPSTEIN: **It's good to see you** Charles. **This is** our Vice-President, Shirley Graham. Shirley, **this is** Charles Blake from Yamashita Ltd.
GRAHAM: **It's nice to meet you,** Mr. Blake.
BLAKE: **Pleased to meet you,** Ms. Graham.
GRAHAM: **How are you today?**
BLAKE: **Fine. And you?**
GRAHAM: Just fine. Mike tells me that . . .

7

EPSTEIN: Well, **I hate to interrupt** but we have a car outside and we have reservations at 12:15. So **why don't we** get over to the restaurant and we can continue our conversation there.
GRAHAM: Okay.
EPSTEIN: Okay?
BLAKE: **That sounds fine** to me.
EPSTEIN: Okay. **Let's go.**
3. **a**

Variations: Introducing Yourself; Looking for Someone
Variation 1: Answer/Transcript

a.; a.; b.; a.

POWERS: Mr. Myers?
MYERS: Yes. **That's right.**
POWERS: **I'm** Sandra Powers. I work with Mr. Malone.
MYERS: Mrs. Powers. **How do you do?** I've been looking forward to meeting you.
POWERS: **It's nice to meet you.** Mr. Myers. You've come a very long way on this trip, so I hope things are going well. Welcome to San Francisco!

Variation 2: Transcript

POWERS: Mr. Myers?
X: **Excuse me?**
POWERS: **Are you** Mr. Myers from Dover Limited?
X: No, **I'm afraid not. Why don't you** ask reception to page him?
POWERS: Oh, thank you. I'll do that. **Sorry to bother you.**
X: Oh, **not at all.**

EPISODE 5   A Business Lunch

A.   Story Update
Transcript

It is now Wednesday, June 12th. It is 1:30 in the afternoon. Mr. Blake, Mr. Epstein, and Ms. Graham are having lunch together at a restaurant. Mr. Blake wants to sell his company's industrial robots to Advanced Technologies. Ms. Graham, of Advanced Technologies, is in charge of a large project to build a new electronics factory. In this factory they will need many industrial robots. Mr. Epstein thinks that the robots made by Yamashita Ltd. are the best. Ms. Graham agrees, but she is worried about several other problems. Mr. Blake needs to convince her that these problems can be solved.

D.   General Comprehension
1. F   2. T   3. F   4. T   5. F

E.   Detailed Listening
1. **pretty good; delicious**   2. **spare parts; maintenance**   3. **b.**   4. **quantity; size**   5. **done busir**

Functional Phrases
2. a., d. **Epstein;**   b. **Blake**   c. **Graham.**
3. Check your answers by looking at the transcript.

Transcript

EPSTEIN: Well, that was a pretty good meal.

8

GRAHAM:	Um, it was delicious.
EPSTEIN:	**Would anyone like** some . . . some more coffee? Shirley?
GRAHAM:	**Not for me.** No, thank you.
BLAKE:	Yes. **I'd like** a little bit more please.
EPSTEIN:	Okay. There's the waiter. Waiter, **could we** get another cup of coffee over here, please. Thank you.

H. Functional Phrases 2

1. a. **confirm**   b. **clarify**   c. **qualify**

2. Okay Ms. Graham, **let me see if I understand you correctly on this**.

3. He has understood that Shirley Graham's basic problem is to do with maintenance and spare parts, but he thinks that she has completely rejected his proposal for Yamashita to use Advanced Technologies' warehouse. She has not completely rejected that proposal. (See transcript.)

4. **Let me clarify that** . . .

5. 1. **c.**,   2. **a.**,   3. **b.**

Transcript

EPSTEIN:	Well, that was a pretty good meal.
GRAHAM:	Um, it was delicious.
EPSTEIN:	**Would anyone like some** . . . some more coffee? Shirley?
GRAHAM:	**Not for me.** No, thank you.
BLAKE:	Yes. **I'd like** a little bit more please.
EPSTEIN:	Okay. There's the waiter. Waiter, **could we** get another cup of coffee over here, please. Thank you.
BLAKE:	Okay, Ms. Graham, **let me see if I understand you correctly on this**. Now your basic problem is that we at Yamashita cannot provide adequate maintenance or spare parts quickly enough.
GRAHAM:	Yes. **That's right.** That's my main concern.
BLAKE:	Okay. Now you've rejected the proposal that we use your warehouse for storage space for spare parts.
GRAHAM:	Well, **not entirely**, Mr. Blake. **Let me clarify that** a little. Space is limited and it would depend very much on the quantity of parts, the size etcetera. I would need a lot more detail on that.
BLAKE:	I can certainly understand your concerns. I'm going to put this information in a report after I fax Tokyo.
GRAHAM:	Okay.
BLAKE:	And I'll have a report ready for you tomorrow. And maybe we can come up with a solution to the problem.
GRAHAM:	Okay. Well, that sounds fine. Even then Mr. Blake, I can't make any guarantees. You know we've never done business with a Japanese company before so it's quite an undertaking.
BLAKE:	Oh, I can certainly understand.
GRAHAM:	So I hope you will understand.
BLAKE:	Sure.
GRAHAM:	Okay.

Variation: Negotiating

1. **The end.** We can tell this from Davis' phrase **To summarize**.
2. **Two: delivery date and size of discount.**
3. **Take action on: delivery date**. They will meet again to discuss this.

Functional Phrases/Transcript

DAVIS: **To summarize**, there are still problems with the delivery date and the size of the discount, but everything else is okay, is that right?

JONES: Yes. **That's right.** The price is higher than we expected, and we need delivery within six months at the latest.

DAVIS: I see. Well, **I'll see what I can do.** The delivery date is going to be a problem, but **I'll check** and see if it's possible. **Can we get together** again? **How about** later this week?

JONES: Okay, but **I'm afraid** I won't be free except for tomorrow afternoon. **Is that too early?**

DAVIS: No, that'll be fine. How about 3:00?

JONES: Okay, good. I'll see you tomorrow, Mr. Davis.

DAVIS: See you then.

EPISODE 6   The Disagreement

A.   Story Update

Transcript

It is now Wednesday afternoon, June 12th. Mr. Epstein and Ms. Graham have finished their meeting with Mr. Blake. They are now in Ms. Graham's office. They are discussing their meeting with Mr. Blake.

Ms. Graham is worried about doing business with Yamashita. She thinks it would be safer to buy robots from an American company, United Industries. Spare parts and maintenance wouldn't be a problem because the United Industries factory is close, and in the past they have always been reliable. Their technological level, however, is not as high as Yamashita's, and their price is a bit higher.

D.   General Comprehension

1. T   2. T   3. F   4. T   5. F

E.   Detailed Listening

1. b.   2. b.   3. a.   4. c.   5. b.

F.   Functional Phrases

2.

AGREEING	DISAGREEING	GIVING YOUR OPINION
I agree (with you).	I'm sorry, but I'm afraid	I think (we should) . . .
You're right.	(I can't agree).	I feel sure . . .

3. Check your answers by looking at the transcript.

Transcript

GRAHAM: . . . Yes, in Japan. The quality of their product is extremely good but I don't know anything about their reliability. Can they be relied on to do this by October 1st? **You know** we've worked with United Industries before and **I think we should** just go ahead on the deal with them. **I feel sure** they can have everything installed and working by October 1st.

EPSTEIN: Well, look, **but there's another argument**, Shirley, and that is that **I agree with you,** they haven't established themselves in the States **but** that's an advantage . . . . that's our advantage because we can get their technology before other companies can. If we're willing to take the risk. **I think we really have to** take that risk.

GRAHAM: Well, **I think** basically that's what it comes down to Mike. You want to take the risk and I really am not willing to. **I don't feel** I can afford to take the risk.

EPSTEIN: Oh, but what have I been doing for the last year? I've been looking for the new technology to really make this factory something special and I think that this is what we need to do. **I can't understand why** you disagree with this. It's very clear.

GRAHAM: And I think **you've done a very good job** but **I think** that there are more disadvantages than advantages. And **I'm sorry but I'm afraid** on this you're just not going to be able to have it the way you want it.

4. Strong recommendation: **a b c**   More tentative recommendation: **d e**

5. Possible answers:
   a. I can understand your reservations, but really, I don't think there's any need to worry.
   b. I think you've got a good argument there, but I'm afraid we're just not going to be able to do it that way.

Variation: Making a Choice

Answers/Transcript

1. **b.**   2. **c.**   3. **a.**   4. **d.**

MALONE: I think we should hire John Hart. He has ten years of experience and he's 35 years old, quite mature. What do you think?

POWERS: I don't agree. I think we should hire Kevin Ward. He's much better educated, and very bright.

MALONE: Yes, he does have an MBA degree, but he doesn't have any real job experience.

POWERS: That's true, but Mr. Hart has only four years' experience in sales.

MALONE: Yes, that's a good point. Maybe we need more information. Let's talk with them both again.

POWERS: Do you really think that's necessary? A second interview is a good idea, but I don't think we have the time. I think we really have to decide today.

MALONE: Well, I agree, time is a problem. But this new position is very important. We can wait one more day. Would you mind calling them back?

POWERS: All right. I'll try to schedule them both for tomorrow afternoon.

EPISODE 7   Keeping in Touch

A.   Story Update

Transcript

It is Thursday afternoon, June 13th. Mr. Epstein and Mr. Blake are in Epstein's office. They have just finished a meeting with Ms. Graham. At that meeting, Blake gave a report to Ms. Graham with a proposal to further discount the price of the robots. In addition, Yamashita would send two engineers to Advanced Technologies. They would provide training in how to service the robots. A large number of spare parts, however, would have to be stored by Advanced Technologies. Ms. Graham was pleased with Blake's report, but she decided not to buy robots from Yamashita.

   Mr. Epstein disagrees with Graham's decision, and he is thinking about resigning. He feels that Advanced Technologies will not succeed if it is not willing to take risks. He thinks it is a mistake not to have the very best technology in the new factory. He hopes to keep in touch with Mr. Blake for future possibilities.

C.   General Comprehension

1. F   2. T   3. F   4. T   5. F

D.   Detailed Listening

1. **c.**   2. **b.**   3. **b.**   4. **a.**   5. **b.**

E. Functional Phrases

1. a. **request**   b. **qualify**   c. **give opinion**   d. **express disappointment**
   e. **accept**   f. **invite**
   i. **express disappointment**   ii. **accept**   iii. **qualify**   iv. **request**   v. **invite**
   vi. **give opinion**
2. Check your answers by looking at the transcript.

Transcript

EPSTEIN: Well, **it's too bad** but **I guess** things worked out the way we thought they might.

BLAKE: Yeah, but this has been a valuable experience for us. Now we know what our biggest problem will be with the North American market.

EPSTEIN: Well for me, of course, I'm still not happy. **I think** your machinery is the best on the market. **It's just too bad** that I . . . we couldn't convince Shirley. **Still,** I can understand her point too. She's under a lot of pressure here to get this . . . this new operation going by October.

BLAKE: Sure.

EPSTEIN: Well listen, what are your plans from here?

BLAKE: Well, tomorrow I'm flying to New York in the afternoon to meet with some prospective customers.

EPSTEIN: Well, I certainly wish you the best of luck out there.

BLAKE: Well, thank you.

EPSTEIN: Also, **I'd like to ask, if you just could** keep in touch later. I'm very interested to know what happens. In the future, you know, we never know what's going to happen but it may be possible for us to work together.

BLAKE: Okay, **I certainly will** Mike.

EPSTEIN: One other thing. **What are you doing** this afternoon?

BLAKE: Well, I have no plans.

EPSTEIN: Well, I remember the nice game of golf that we had together when I was in Tokyo. I have a membership in a golf club just across the Bay here and I've made some reservations. **Would you like to join me** in a round of golf this afternoon?

BLAKE: **That sounds like a great idea.** Sure.

EPSTEIN: Good the weather's fine.

BLAKE: Okay. Let's go.

EPSTEIN: Great. I'd just love to get out of this office today.

BLAKE: Great.

EPSTEIN: Let's go.

Variation: Making a Polite Refusal

Answers/Transcript

1. **To look around their company's factory.**
   To join her for lunch.
2. **He says he has other appointments.**
3. **No, because he does not want to do business with her.**

WINTHROP: I'd like to invite you (**Would you like**) to see our factory while you are in New York.

VALE: That's very kind of you. But I'm afraid (**Unfortunately,**) my schedule is booked up all next week.

WINTHROP: That's too bad. (**I'm sorry to hear that.**) Well, let's keep in touch. (**I'd like to keep in touch.**) I may be in London early next year and . . .

VALE: Okay. Please give me a call.

WINTHROP: Thank you. I'll do that. (**I certainly will.**) Well, it's nearly 12:30. Why don't you join me (**Are you free**) for lunch?

VALE: I'm sorry but (**I'm afraid I'm not.**) I have other plans. Thank you anyway. (**I appreciate the invitation.**)

WINTHROP: Not at all. (**My pleasure.**) Perhaps another time.

EPISODE 8   New Customer

A.   Story Update

Transcript

It is Monday, June 17th. Mr. Blake has left San Francisco and is now in New York. He is scheduled to meet with Mr. Stewart Chapman of Federal Motors this morning. Mr. Chapman is a systems engineer and is a Vice-President at Federal Motors.

Federal Motors is an automobile company. It is a very large company, and it is now modernizing its present factories. Mr. Chapman is very interested in Yamashita's robots, and he has studied the technical information that was sent to him from Yamashita. He is impressed by Yamashita's high technology, and he is looking forward to meeting with Mr. Blake.

Mr. Blake has just arrived at the Federal Motors building in New York City. He has an appointment with Mr. Stewart Chapman to discuss the possibility of selling industrial robots to Federal Motors.

C.   General Comprehension

1. F   2. T   3. F   4. T   5. F

D.   Detailed Listening

1. b.   2. c.   3. a.   4. b.   5. b.

E.   Functional Phrases

1.   ON THE PHONE: **a., b., d., f., g., h., i., j.**
     FACE-TO-FACE: **b., c., d., e., g., h., k., l., m**
     BOTH: **b., d., g., h.**

2.   Check your answers by looking at the transcript.

Transcript

RECEPTIONIST:	Good morning sir, **can I help you?**
BLAKE:	Yeah, **I have an appointment** to see Mr. Chapman, Stewart Chapman at 10:30.
RECEPTIONIST:	Oh, Mr. Chapman. **Can I have your name please?**
BLAKE:	Yeah, **the name** is Blake, Charles Blake of Yamashita Limited.
RECEPTIONIST:	All right, thank you. Just a moment please . . . Yes, there's a Mr. Blake here to see Mr. Chapman . . . Oh, I see, thank you . . . Uh, Mr. Blake, I'm sorry, Mr. Chapman is not here today.
BLAKE:	Uh-huh . . .
RECEPTIONIST:	But there's a Mr. Gomez who can come talk to you. Would you take a chair and wait for a moment?
BLAKE:	Okay, sure. Thank you.
RECEPTIONIST:	Thank you.
GOMEZ:	Good morning Mr. Blake. **Welcome to** Federal Motors. My name is Dave Gomez.
BLAKE:	**Pleased to meet you** Mr. Gomez.
GOMEZ:	Nice to meet you, sir. Did you have a good trip to New York?
BLAKE:	Yeah, and I'm looking forward to staying here for a few days and doing some business.

3.   **Probably to show him as much respect as possible. Remember that Charles Blake was hoping to see Mr. Chapman.**

4. Confident: **b., f.**   Becoming more tentative: **a., d.**   Very tentative: **c., e.**
5. Check your answers by looking at the transcript.

Transcript

GOMEZ: Great. Uh, Mr. Chapman asked me to apologize to you. He was called out of town on a personal matter very suddenly. And he does assure me he is looking forward to meeting with you as soon as he gets back.
BLAKE: Uh-huh.
GOMEZ: In the meantime, I'm quite familiar with Yamashita and your products, and so **I'd like to** work with you **if that would be all right**?
BLAKE: Okay, sure. And **I understand** about Mr. Chapman's absence. **It's no problem.**
GOMEZ: Great. Uh, you must be tired from your trip. **Why don't we** go into the office and sit down and relax for a few minutes and we can get some coffee or tea **if you'd like**?
BLAKE: Okay, that sounds great.
GOMEZ: Great.

6. **He is probably disappointed.**
   His first response is **Uh-huh** which doesn't sound very polite. He later gives a better response when he says **I understand about Mr. Chapman's absence. It's no problem.**

Variation: Asking a Favor
Transcript

MALONE: **Hello.**
POWERS: Hello, Bill. Sorry to call you at home.
MALONE: **No problem. What can I do for you?**
POWERS: I'm afraid I've got a problem. My mother is quite ill and I have to fly to Miami today. I hate to ask, but would you mind meeting Bob Myers of Dover Limited, tomorrow?
MALONE: **I'm sorry to hear about your mother. I'd be happy to help out. What time do you expect Mr. Myers to arrive?**
POWERS: He'll be there at 10:30.
MALONE: **Okay, I'll meet him then.**
POWERS: Thanks. Again, I'd like to apologize for this inconvenience.
MALONE: **Don't worry about it. I'll take care of everything here and I certainly hope your mother is feeling better.**
POWERS: Thank you. I hope I can be back by Wednesday, but I'm just not sure right now.
MALONE: **Sure, I understand.**
POWERS: Thanks again. I appreciate it. I'll call you tomorrow afternoon around 4:00.
MALONE: **Fine, I'll talk with you then.**

EPISODE 9   Negotiations

A.   Story Update

1. **Meeting with Gomez is on Tuesday, June 18th, not Wednesday, June 19th.**
2. **Chapman is due back on Wednesday, June 19th.**

Transcript

It is now Tuesday, June 18th. Mr. Chapman is still out of town and won't be back until tomorrow, so Mr. Blake is meeting with Dave Gomez. Yesterday they discussed the technology of the robots, the price, and a little about how the robots are being used by other companies in Japan. In general, Mr. Gomez was very impressed.

There are still several problems that need to be discussed. Mr. Blake is worried, because some of these problems are the same problems that forced Advanced Technologies to decide not to buy from Yamashita. On the other hand, one point in his favor is that there isn't as much time pressure as before. Federal Motors won't need the robots for about six months. Mr. Blake and Mr. Gomez have been talking for about an hour and a half. They are now reviewing several important points in the negotiations.

D. General Comprehension

1. F   2. F   3. T   4. F   5. T

E. Detailed Listening

1. b.   2. b.   3. b.   4. c.   5. c.

6.

POINTS RAISED (Dave Gomez)	SOLUTIONS (Charles Blake)
1. Need group of English-speaking technical engineers to train workforce.	Send over engineers who are in an English Language training program now.
2. Need clear and easy to read service manual in English.	Manual in preparation now.
3. Need information about Yamashita's performance record.	Send reports from Japanese client companies.

F. Functional Phrases

1. a. vii.   b. iv.   c. viii.   d. iii.   e. vi.   f. ii.   g. i.   h. v.
2. Check your answers by looking at the transcript.

Transcript

GOMEZ: When we first put these machines in operation, we install them in our factories, can you send over a group of technical advisors who speak English and could train our engineers and workmen?

BLAKE: Certainly. In fact we have some engineers in a language training program now. They could come over within a few months and be available any time you need them.

GOMEZ: Great, great, that sounds good. Another one of our major concerns is the service manual. We're quite concerned about getting a service manual in English that will be easy to read and very clear and useful for our engineers.

BLAKE: Yeah. Again, **as I told you** we are preparing a translation of the Japanese manual we have now, and we expect that to be ready in a short time.

GOMEZ: By a short time . . . **could you give me** an estimate?

BLAKE: Uh, I'd like to say two weeks, **but I'd have to get back to you**, but probably about two or three weeks.

GOMEZ: **Oh, that sounds quite reasonable.** As you know we have until January 1st to actually install these machines and get them operating, so we're under no deadline pressure here.

BLAKE: Okay, well that gives us a fair amount of time to work with.

GOMEZ: Plenty of time. That sounds good, Mr. Blake. Uh, another concern is your professional record-uh-performance record in Japan with these machines.

BLAKE: **Why don't I** send you some reports that we have on the performance of the robot in some Japanese companies who are also our clients. And I'm sure you'll be quite pleased with what you see.

GOMEZ: Okay, great. Could you get those off to me within a few weeks?

BLAKE: Sure. **That shouldn't be a problem.** In fact, as soon as I get back to Tokyo **I'll see to it.**

GOMEZ: Excellent. Uh, thank you very much.

BLAKE: **Is there anything else?**

GOMEZ: Well, no. That covers all the major points.

BLAKE: Okay. Fine.
GOMEZ: Sounds good . . .

Variations: Telling someone there have been changes

Variation 1: Answers/Transcript

CHARLES: **Hello, this is Charles Blake speaking.**
MIKE: Charles. This is Mike Epstein.
CHARLES: **Oh. Hi, Mike, how are you?**
MIKE: Well that's why I'm calling you., There have been some changes here, and I wanted to let you know.
CHARLES: **What kind of changes?**
MIKE: Well, Shirley Graham has resigned, and I've been put in charge of our project.
CHARLES: **Well, I'm sorry to hear about Shirley, but congratulations to you.**
MIKE: Thank you. But that's not all. I'm still interested in getting your machines for our new factory, and I've been able to extend the deadline for a month, to November 1st. Do you think you can make it?
CHARLES: **Well, if you can accept my earlier proposal, I don't see any problem.**
MIKE: When are you flying back to Tokyo?
CHARLES: **Tomorrow morning.**
MIKE: Could you change your flight and stop by here for a day or two?
CHARLES: **Let me check with my office in Tokyo first, then I'll get back to you.**
MIKE: If you could call me back within a couple of hours and let me know, I'd appreciate it.
CHARLES: **Well, our office in Tokyo doesn't open for another four hours** . . .
MIKE: Right. I forgot about the time difference . . .

Variation 2: Answers/Transcript

The correct order is:
i. m. n. h. o. g. f. d. l. e. a. c. k. j. b. p.

BLAKE: Yes? This is Charles Blake speaking.
EPSTEIN: Hello Charles. This is Mike Epstein calling.
BLAKE: Oh, Mike, it's good to hear from you. What's up?
EPSTEIN: Well, to begin with, I've decided to leave Advanced Technologies and join another company. I've been thinking about it for quite a while now, and last week I was offered a position at Data Systems Inc.
BLAKE: Well, congratulations.
EPSTEIN: Thanks. But the reason I'm calling you is that I'll be working on a project very similar to the one I was working on before, and there's a good chance that we'll be interested in your machines.
BLAKE: Well, that's great news. I'll be looking forward to hearing from you.
EPSTEIN: If you could keep me informed of any new development, I'd really appreciate it.
BLAKE: I'll certainly do that.
EPSTEIN: How did things go in New York?
BLAKE: Well we just finished our meeting, and things look very good. They like our technology, and there are no serious problems. Some of their people will fly to Tokyo the week after next, and if things work out, I'm pretty sure we'll get our first big order in North America. I'm very pleased.
EPSTEIN: Well, congratulations. Next time we get together, we'll have to celebrate.
BLAKE: Sounds good Mike. And maybe we'll even get in a round of golf.
EPSTEIN: Good idea. Well, have a good trip back to Tokyo, Charles.
BLAKE: Thanks for calling, and good luck with your new job.
EPSTEIN: Thanks.